HUME PAPERS ON PUBLIC POLICY·
Volume 6

ESSAYS, MORAL
AND ECON
Samuel Brittan

D0537647

D

THE DAVID HUME INSTITUTE

Hume Papers on Public Policy
Volume 6 No 4 Winter 1998

ESSAYS, MORAL, POLITICAL AND ECONOMIC
Samuel Brittan

EDINBURGH UNIVERSITY PRESS

© The David Hume Institute 1998

Edinburgh University Press
22 George Square, Edinburgh

Typeset in Times by WestKey Limited,
Falmouth, Cornwall
Printed and bound in Great Britain by
Page Bros Ltd, Norwich, Norfolk

A CIP record for this book is available
from the British Library

ISBN 0 7486 1208 4

Contents

Foreword

It was a fortunate day for The David Hume Institute when Sir Samuel Brittan agreed to become its President. His learning and gift of lucid exposition exemplify the Institute's goals, and he has been prepared to put both at our disposal in this fascinating and very timely collection of revised versions of his recent work. Sir Samuel himself provides an overview of the essential thrust of that work in the Introduction which immediately follows this Foreword, so we shall not attempt a summary here. Suffice it to say that Brittan expounds an individualist vision of liberalism which welcomes some of the New Labour policy initiatives, but rejects its communitarian rhetoric as well as its authoritarian echoes on the Right. This vision forms the context in which a number of current issues are discussed: the globalisation of the economy, the future of state-provided welfare, and the control of inflation among them. Sir Samuel does not limit himself to critical analysis of the past and the present; he sets out an agenda for the future in which are combined idealism and realism. He frequently invokes the spirit and thought of David Hume in this respect. The David Hume Institute is delighted to provide the means of bringing together Sir Samuel's thought-provoking, indeed provocative, analyses, although as ever remaining independent of the views expressed.

Hector L MacQueen and Brian G M Main
Editors, *Hume Papers on Public Policy*

Essays: Moral, Political and Economic
Introduction

Blairism and New Labour

It is a matter of luck for those of us who believe that competitive capitalism is the least bad economic system available that Labour elected a leader who shared such belief – even though combined with oratorical embellishments about a "third way" – and yet who still managed to maintain control of his party. The electorate has thus had a better government than it deserves. For Labour would have almost certainly won the 1997 election on a Michael Foot platform if only the image-makers could have got rid of the famous duffle coat.

Indeed it has often seemed to me that the public ideal of a well-run economy would not be very different from the rule book of former East Germany. Although the Conservatives succeeded in making nationalisation a dirty word, very few people have understood the functions of markets and prices as a way of transmitting information and providing incentives to produce what their fellow citizens want them to produce by the cheapest possible methods. (These intemperate assertions are empirically supported in Brittan, 1973 and 1997).

Yet the avoidance of the worst forms of economic collectivism is not enough to give any government a clean bill of healh. There remain still the threat of moral authoritarianism and the threat of capitalism with an excessively puritan face. When was asked what he thought of the French Revolution, the former Chinese Prime Minister Chou En Lai, replied: "It is far too early to say." This also applies to any assessment of New Labour and the Blair government.

Much of what the government is undertaking marks an advance on the past: not only in the economic field, but – even more important – in constitutional reform and human rights. Yet much of the oratory, obvious well in advance of the 1997 election, has been illiberal and offputting.

My own pet dislike is for the awful communitarian rhetoric. It really is too early to say whether this will remain a sideshow, left to the speech writers, or whether it will ultimately corrupt the substance of policy in ways highlighted in this volume. By contrast the so-called rebranding of the UK or the promotion of the image of cool Britain – although right outside the proper agenda of government – mainly adds to the gaiety of public affairs for a comparatively modest resource cost. So long as it is not taken too seriously.

Looked at with a cold eye, the job of government is to provide those services which are best provided collectively through the tax system, rather than by private enterprise under the market mechanism, or by voluntary co-operation. That is so whether one believes that the list of such collective services is short or long.

The fashionable spin-doctoring view of government points to a different function altogether. It is to provide so-called moral leadership. (Some of us still remember Dick the Vicar from *Beyond the Fringe*). It is also to reflect "the more optimistic trends in our society", e.g. Tony Blair's talk about Britain being a young country. There is undoubtedly a place both for role models and for preachers. But these are not necessarily functions of government. There is is a lot to be said for Harold Macmillan's remark that if people were seeking a moral lead they should look to the archbishops rather than to politicians.

The main body of this book does say something about the danger of too much political moralism. But for the most part it deals with issues more basic than the foibles of particular governments.

Content

It has long been my wish to publish some essays without having to fabricate a headline slogan for a title. Such titles might be pleasing to publishers, but they can at best give a very partial idea of content. My tenure as President of the David Hume Institute has emboldened me to follow the example of the illustrious philosopher after whom the Institute is named.

Hume entitled his work in this genre *Essays, Moral and Political* and *Essays: Moral, Political and Literary* in different editions. I have been bold enough to adopt a variant, *Essays, Moral, Political and Economic*. The intention is not of course to invite comparisons but to borrow from Hume's insights in the minor matter of titles and to pay him tribute. Needless to say, I am using the word moral in its eighteenth-century sense to cover any aspect of the study of human behaviour.

As on previous occasions, I soon realised that essays and addresses written for different purposes and at different times required a good deal of editing if they were to be read as a whole. My aim has been to reduce overlapping and present the material in coherent order, but without losing the flavour of the original occasion. Some of the chapters such as Three and Nine, were very obviously prepared for oral delivery and I have retained the lecture form. The footnote attributions for each chapter are meant not only to provide some context but to thank those who first gave me the opportunity to outline the ideas expressed and, where necessary, gave me permission to reproduce the material. I am particularly grateful to the John Stuart Mill Institute, which gave a trial run to the first three chapters in a pamphlet entitled *Towards a Humane Individualism*, published early in 1998.

The chapter titles are meant to be self-explanatory and to avoid the cuteness and forced jocularity of American-style blockbusters. The aim of Part I is to rescue individualism from its identification with mere selfishness and to bring it into contact with mainstream liberal thought – liberal with a small "l". It has also the negative task of showing what is wrong with slogans about communitarianism and supposed third ways between liberal market capitalism on the one hand and collectivism on the other. My strictures on the propaganda in favour of the so-called Asian model were written before the financial crisis that hit East Asian economies late in 1997 and do not depend on that crisis for their validity.

The more domestic discussion of communitarian economics is choke-full of misplaced moralism. An example is the vogue for "stakeholding". If the word means anything at all, it is that the managers of a business should have some other aim in mind than gaining the maximum return from the assets under their control. I find it difficult to see what the nation gains from not using assets to their best advantage. Remember that the owners do not have to be anonymous shareholders. They can be the workers themselves under ESOP (Employee Share Ownership Plan) arrangements.

Part II deals with subjects on which I might be expected to have something to say as an economic journalist. Public discussion here is full of what I call Lumpeneconomics. The slightly archaic German word "Lumpen" means rags and tatters. Lumpeneconomics is a second rate substitutes for genuine economic thinking. Just as under some circumstances bad money drives out good, so bad thinking may drive out good thinking.

Lumpeneconomics is particularly widespread in discussion of the bogey of globalisation, covered in Chapter Six. But the distribution of material in this Part is inevitably slightly arbitrary as some topics belong to nearly all the chapters. The future of the welfare state, discussed in Chapter Seven, is of course being intensively debated and the government is committed to changes. I have therefore had to be very selective rather than comprehensive. Chapter Eight deals with monetary, fiscal and exchange rate policy, which are widely but wrongly believed to be the whole of economics. I found I still had something to add, as the present practices of governments and central banks are not yet the last word in human wisdom.

The obvious omission from Part II is European Monetary Union. A key set of decisions is due to be taken while this book is in the press and there is no advantage to be gained from trying to jump the gun. Readers who suspect that I have funked the issue are reminded that the David Hume Institute has already been kind enough to publish an analysis of mine of the more durable arguments under the title *A Cool Look at the Euro* (1997). Other readers may believe that the subject has already has been flogged to death. The important economic reason for UK membership used to be that here was the most likely method of introducing an independent central bank. But this has already been achieved to a large extent by the Blair government in a domestic context.

The main remaining economic advantage of EMU for Britain is that it would abolish the overshooting and undershooting of sterling, which have led to swings of 30 per cent or more in the exchange rate in recent years and destabilised British overseas trade. It would do so by merging sterling into the euro, leaving only some 10 per cent of GDP affected by swings of the euro against other world currencies such as the dollar and the yen. The disadvantage is that the European Central Bank will have to find one interest rate for an area extending from the Algarve of southern Portugal to the tundra of northern Finland and from Connemara to the Czech borders. It is most unlikely that a rate chosen to meet average EU conditions would be at all similar to that selected by an operationally independent Bank of England with British needs in mind. With the economic case so unclear, it is reasonable to base a vote in an EMU referendum on political instinct.

It is wishful thinking to suppose that by not joining in the starting year of 1999 and waiting another two or three years, the British Government will accumulate enough further evidence on which to base an informed economic judgment. Euro notes and coins will not even be in circulation until well into 2002. Nevertheless it will be all too easy for Eurosceptics to blame any European economic misfortunes on the birth pangs of EMU. It will be equally tempting for Euroenthusiasts to give credit to EMU for events such as business cycle upturns, which may have nothing to do with the euro and would have taken place without it.

In any event, the costs associated with dealing with many different European currencies will disappear if 11 have been merged together. British exporters will then have to bother with only one exchange conversion rather than the dozens of cross rates about which they have to worry at the moment. In that case the UK will be to some extent a free rider on the efforts of its neighbours. Use of the euro by British business is likely to spread even without formal membership of EMU by the British Government. Already several large UK-based international companies are planning to prepare accounts in euros. The result could be the emergence of the euro as a parallel currency competing with sterling in many transactions. There is a partial analogy with Latin American countries and the former Soviet Union which use the dollar to invoice many international and large internal transactions, but stick to domestic currencies for wage payments and ordinary retail business. The process may be slower in Britain without the incentive of rapidly depreciating domestic currencies from which Latin America has so long suffered.

Part III of this book deals with the very slippery idea of cause and effect when applied to economic affairs or, for that matter, history and social sciences generally. As anything in this area which can be misunderstood will be misunderstood, I have added a short book review critical of some versions of the "post-modern" approach.

The concluding Part IV is not the usual manifesto or programme of action – of which we have had too many – but a plea for the study of human affairs as ultimately a branch of biology. For, despite Disraeli's assertion to the contrary, we are in the end more nearly apes than angels. The most promising approach, although certainly not the only one, seems to be Darwinian psychology which has enjoyed a rebirth. But it needs to be assessed just as critically as statements of political and economic theorists.

There are some non-obvious interrelations between the chapters. Chapter Three does go into some details of actual policies, which are taken up again in Chapter Seven on the Welfare State. Some monetary controversies are taken up as examples in Chapter Nine on Causation. Perhaps I should also warn readers that Chapters Four and Eight are in their different ways the most difficult in the book. Chapter Four deals with age old political issues about the distribution of the good things of this world. But the contractarianism which it embraces has been explained in numerous other works, including earlier books of my own, and my object here is to advance the argument rather than to explain it all from the beginning. Chapter Eight is an unsolicited contribution to a conversation taking place in the economic policy community, a conversation in which many citizens have, quite understandably, no desire to participate.

As it is extremely unlikely that any individual writer outside academia (or even in it) will contribute many original insights, my main aim has been to shed fresh light on the existing stock of ideas. The one place where I claim a little originality is in Chapter One where I try to tackle head-on the puzzled hostility generated by Adam Smith's dictum about relying on the self interest of other human beings for our daily bread, and claim that this is best thought of as a less obvious principle of utilitarian morality.

References

Brittan, S., (1973). *Is There an Economic Consensus?* London: Macmillan.
Brittan, S., (1997). Better than you deserve. *Financial Times*, 3 May.

PART I

LIBERAL INDIVIDUALISM

Chapter One
In Defence of Individualism*

Liberals versus Communitarians

There are many writers and critics who regard what they call individualist-liberalism as the root of many of the evils of the modern world; and the emphasis of their attack is on the individualist half of the term. Those who take this line nowadays often call themselves communitarians. I would prefer to call them collectivists, as that brings out their dangerous tendency to regard the group as more important than the individuals of whom it is composed. But in what follows I shall concede on labels and most often refer to them as communitarians. There are a number of slogans characteristic of communitarian rhetoric.

The most frequent of them is that Man is a political (or sometimes social) animal. The individualist-liberal is then accused of an atomistic view of society. Another slogan is that more emphasis should be put on duties instead of rights. Here there would be no difference between Tony Blair and Margaret Thatcher. In a lower key there is a preference for teamwork as opposed to individual responsibility (apparent even in the new UK arrangements for monetary policy).

But the emphasis of the attack is on modern market capitalism. The historian of political thought, C B MacPherson, called this possessive individualism, an expression which has caught on with many who have not read a single word of his work. The more lowbrow version is a contempt for the pursuit of the bottom line which is said to characterise our age. Ordinary citizens are accused of consumerism or of being obsessed by the psychology of "me, me, me".

In Britain the debate is confused because almost everyone on the left and centre now adopts a communitarian rhetoric. Having accepted much of the economic counter-revolution of the last decade and a half, the main issue on which Blairites dig in their heels is opposition to supposed Thatcherite individualism. This is based on a false chain of reasoning which identifies individualism with self-interest and self-interest with selfishness. The last is a howler, as can be testified by anyone who has laboured for a charity, for a good cause or any of the arts or religion or merely to improve the lot of his or her own family and intimates.

*A paper delivered at the Royal Institute of Philosophy Conference, St Andrews, 1997.

Many on the left will wonder why I am putting right-wing authoritarians together with benevolent communitarians. The American debate sheds some light here. A whole movement has risen there to attack the liberal individualist foundations of Western politics and culture. US communitarians dislike almost equally ultra-free market libertarians and the more left-wing liberals, such as the philosopher John Rawls, who support the welfare state and other forms of economic intervention. Communitarians condemn them both for regarding the individual person and his or her choices as the measure of all things in politics, and their failure to find a higher purpose for government.

The softer version of US communitarianism can be found in the writings of commentators such as Amital Etzioni, who is pictured with Vice President Al Gore on the dust cover of his book, *The Spirit of Community*. Its harder version can be found in the Republican Religious Right, with its support of compulsory religious practices (of which school prayer is but a symbol), belief in savage punishment for retributive reasons and paranoid nationalist fears that foreigners are taking away American jobs.

The two kinds of anti-individualists come together in their advocacy of a year or two of compulsory national service to knock some patriotism and civic virtue into the American young. They have been answered by an individualist liberal, David Boaz, who replies:

> No group of people has the right to force another group to give up a year or two of their lives – and possibly life itself – without their consent. The basic liberal principle of the dignity of the individual is violated when individuals are treated as national resources.

Another tell-tale symptom is propaganda for so-called Asian values and admiration for the Singaporean leader Lee Kuan Yew, who justifies his brutal punishments by saying, "To us in Asia, an individual is an ant". Are British Conservatives more tolerant? Almost every increase in personal liberty and toleration, from the legalisation of homosexuality among consenting adults to the abolition of theatre censorship and more sensible divorce laws, has been brought about in the face of opposition from the majority of Conservative MPs and activists. In nearly every country the political Right (with a few honourable individual exceptions) is adamantly opposed to any re-examination of the drug laws which have done so much to make money-laundering one of the world's biggest businesses. Their text is still that of Lord Hailsham 40 years ago when he hoped that the addicts of hashish and marijuana would be pursued with the utmost severity the law allowed. He hoped they would find themselves in the Old Bailey, where, "however distinguished their positions in the Top 10, they will be treated as criminals deserve to be treated". Unfortunately, too many Blairites rush to show their political moderation by coming down like a ton of bricks on anyone on the Labour or Liberal side who opposes such Hailshamite blusterings.

The Academic Debate

The communitarian-liberal debate has been going on in the USA for a decade or more; and two Oxford philosophers, S Mulhall and A Swift, have recently written a textbook guide to it. This takes as its starting point John Rawls's *Theory of Justice*, which has acquired a canonical status and which I shall not attempt to summarise here. Many individualist-liberals have criticised Rawls for making too many concessions to collectivist goals. But the communitarian attack is just the opposite. It is on the priority which Rawls says he attaches to personal freedom.

The debate takes place on several levels. What seems to motivate Alasdair McIntyre and those who think like him is an intense hostility to theories in philosophical ethics such as emotivism, subjectivism and relativism. Such philosophers insist that some ways of life are preferable to others and are incensed by Jeremy Bentham's observation that Push-pin (an early nineteenth-century board game) was better than poetry if that was what people preferred. Today the argument would be in terms of Radio One versus Radio Three. But these philosophers are not necessarily committed to the specific proposals urged by more policy-oriented commmunitarians who are looking for some third way between socialism and market capitalism.

Metaphysical Anti-individualism

In my experience, communitarians like to start from some metaphysical proposition. They say for instance that an individual is constituted by his or her social relationships. He or she is a grandfather, a doctor, a member of certain clubs, an active Scottish Nationalist, and so on. Without these relation-ships he or she is said to be nothing. Even a hermit is identified by his decision to abandon the community from which he springs. (One often reads that the individual was an invention of the Renaissance and was unknown to the ancient and mediaeval world. I am not sure that this can be reconciled with the funeral oration of Pericles, as expounded by Thucydides.)

We soon get into an impasse. Groups are made up of individuals; but individuals form groups. A debate on which fact is primary is the kind of dispute which never gets settled. As Stephen Holmes has pointed out:

> The social nature of Man is too trite to count as an insight and is worthless as an argument for or against any existing institutional arrangements. If all individuals are socially constituted then the social self cannot serve as a critical standard to praise some societies and revile others.

A Biological Perspective

Communitarians are inclined to say that the issue depends on the nature of Man. To my mind this a biological matter rather than one for armchair speculation. And you do not escape the biological nature of the problem by talking in seemingly more philosophical terms of the nature of the person instead. It is a cliche to say Man is a social animal. The statement can be given empirical content by noting that for the greater part of his existence on this planet he has belonged to clans of hunter-gatherers of not more than a couple of hundred people. It is, therefore, not surprising that people feel alienated, both in mass society and if left entirely to their own devices in nuclear families. This could be held to support the communitarian preference for relying on, whenever possible, local groups rather than the isolated individual or the nation state. Communitarians are, however, seldom specific about how this transfer can be undertaken.

Let us, moreover, not romanticise the small group. It can be very oppressive and stultifying; and even in primitive times there were those who left their groups to start other clans. Many of today's most vibrant communities are not people who are geographically close to each other. The most important communities for users of the Internet in the Orkneys may consist, not of village neighbours, but other users with whom they form a professional link which can blossom into friendship and mutual support.

The worst side of group psychology is the hostility almost always generated to those outside the group. This long predates modern nationalism. Byzantine emperors were able to generate artificial hostility between groups of citizens by dividing them by an arbitrary line into blues and greens. From here it is but a short distance to the bitter struggles in places like Bosnia, where people who had previously lived at ease with each other for generations, and indeed intermarried, went in for the barbarities of ethnic cleansing.

Many of the achievements of civilisation are due to what Graham Wallas, the Fabian sociologist, called the great society. This was the linking together through the market process of millions who have no chance of being personally acquainted. One interpretation of globalisation is that the whole world is becoming a great society. The problem ever since the Industrial Revolution, if not earlier, has been how to combine the benefits of the great society with the human ties generated by the smaller group.

Defensible Individualism

In current political polemics individualism is a pejorative term used by opponents of the concept. Few political writers call themselves individualists. They are more likely to say they are classical liberals, market liberals, old-fashioned liberals or something of the kind. But there clearly is an individualist component of their beliefs which is worth defending. The kind of individualism for which I will fight in the last ditch is ethical individualism. In its minimal form, it is the belief that actions should be judged by their effects on individual human beings.

How would I justify this judgement? It is individuals who feel, exult, despair and rejoice. And statements about group welfare are a shorthand way of referring to such individual effects. This seems to me a plain statement of fact, despite the numerous thinkers who deny – or more usually – bypass it. Whatever might be said about sharing feelings with a close member of one's family, the rejoicing of a nation or a football club or a school is metaphorical.

The danger of collectivism is that of attributing a superior value to collective entities over and above the individuals who compose it. This disastrous error was made respectable by the teachings of Hegel and reached its apotheosis in the state worship of the Nazi and Communist regimes. But it is lurking behind even the apparently more soft-hearted varieties of communitarianism.

Statements about large abstractions such as the interests of a country and the health of the economy must be translatable into statements about individual human beings. This translation cannot logically prevent the collectivist judgements I find so repellent; but such translations can nevertheless lead us to pose useful questions such as: How much suffering is justified by the gratification of my feelings of national pride as a Serb or a Croat? Analysis along such lines would be likely to make people more self-conscious. It might even lead to a weakening of unreflective willingness to die for one's country, or the working class, and to a waning of nationalism and ideological enthusiasm in general.

Going beyond this reductionism, we do not find a single individualist creed. Benthamite utilitarianism does involve a commitment to individual welfare, but not to personal freedom. (The inhabitants of Aldous Huxley's *Brave New World* were made to take their soma pills.) Post-Bentham, individualists from John Stuart Mill onwards, argued for the largest possible measure of individual freedom consistent with avoiding harm to others. They did so formally on the grounds that individuals were less bad judges of their own interests than governments, experts or others who claimed to judge. But it is pretty clear from reading the classical liberals that they valued freedom for its own sake.

What is so wonderful about individual choice? One can only reply that it lies in the absence of coercion or man-made obstacles to the exercise of people's powers and capacities. In the final analysis, this judgement cannot be demonstrated rigorously against those with incompatibly different values. One can only try to remove misunderstandings and to display by anecdote, rhetoric and imaginative literature the virtues of the kind of society in which people have maximum opportunity to satisfy their preferences against societies where others make their judgements for them.

A particular misunderstanding is to pit the individual against the family. Anthropology and biology suggest that human beings are creatures who tend to live in one kind of family or another. The individualist is, however, more content to let the family evolve and hesitates to put a political imprimatur on the nuclear family in the state it reached among the middle classes of the late nineteenth century. Nevertheless, the liberal-individualist passion for choice is always tempered by the proviso that it must not harm others; and, if the break-up of traditional families is having the adverse effects on individual welfare which Melanie Phillips claims, governments need to take such factors into account in legislation. However important the family, one is still allowed to write on other matters. And it is surely clear that it is not families but collective entities, from the state down to local collections of busybodies, from which the individualists want to protect us.

Self-realisation

Individualists usually desire to go beyond liberating human beings from collectivist pressures and want to celebrate the achievements of particular people, whether in the arts or sciences or sports, or in the more mundane art of everyday living. This kind of positive individualism has its antithesis in the idealisation of the team. Indeed, it is the British focus on team spirit which heavily qualifies the romantic continental notion that they are a nation of individualists.

Recently I had occasion to congratulate an economist friend on some well-deserved professional promotion. He thanked me very generously, saying how glad he was that the work of his team had been recognised. But this is not what I meant at all. I was expressing pleasure that he personally had been promoted and that the choice had not been made on political grounds.

To go further into the more positive and indeed romantic aspects of individualism would take a separate paper. This would have to recognise the danger of this form of individualism becoming converted into worship of great men, such as Napoleon or Frederick the Great, for whom the lives and welfare of millions are sacrificed. Even in everyday life rugged individualism sometimes means a craggy disregard for other people's interests, which is not a quality I wish to celebrate.

Political Economy

A point requiring some emphasis is that an ethical individualist does not have to be an economic individualist. Generations of socialists have indeed argued that the collective control of economic activity would not only enable more individual citizens to satisfy more of their wants, but would enable them to flourish in a broader way.

The argument against collectivist economic systems is that they utterly fail to fulfil their promise. Of course, it is a bonus to the individualist that allowing some rein to individual instincts for self-betterment will produce better results than centrally imposed direction. Nevertheless, the test of Adam Smith's view of the superiority of Natural Liberty must be that of experiments thrown up by events and not just of its psychological attractiveness or otherwise.

Just as a philosophical individualist does not have to be an economic individualist, the same distinction works the other way round. An economic individualist does not have to share a wider individualist philosophy. He or she may simply accept that a market-based economic system brings better results without having a deeper belief in individual choice or in people "doing their own thing".

Exponents of free markets often oppose freedom in every other sphere, especially in sexual behaviour and the behaviour of the young. This combination of economic individualism with authoritarian wider beliefs is all too common among many Conservatives, even in the so-called Thatcherite wing of that party.

Economic Individualism

Despite these disclaimers, the type of individualism which is most under a cloud is economic individualism. It is associated with slogans like "It's every man for himself and let the devil take the hindmost". Or with Charles Dickens' Mr Gradgrind (his name, not the actual character in *Hard Times*). Or with thick-skinned City types who celebrate the rat-race in which they boast they are engaged. Even if the collapse of collectivist economic systems leaves people with no alternative, this fact is regarded as a necessary evil rather than anything to celebrate.

The greatest obstacle faced by economic individualism is the belief that it is based on, or encourages, materialism or acquisitiveness. In fact, self-interest in a market economy merely means that people follow their own chosen goals. These may be individual consumption; but they may equally be the acquiring of means to promote charitable, cultural or religious causes. Or they may try to maximise leisure to pursue some hobby or interest; or some mixture of all these. The altruistic businessman should indeed strive harder than his rivals to make profits and differentiate himself by what he does with his gain.

These necessary elaborations only take us a certain way. Defenders of market capitalism have rarely faced up to the shock with which many well brought-up people react when they learn that their job is not to feed or clothe, or even entertain, their fellow citizens directly, but to promote the profits of the company's owners. That is irrespective of how worthy or unworthy are the purposes to which the profits are devoted.

The most controversial aspect of economic individualism was expressed two centuries ago, by Adam Smith. No sentence in political thought has attracted more opprobrium than the passage in *The Wealth of Nations* saying:

> It is not from the benevolence of the butcher, brewer or baker that we expect our dinner, but from the regard to their own interest. We address ourselves, not to their humanity but to their self love, and never talk to them of our own necessities but of their advantages.

The moralist is not appeased to learn that Smith also wrote *The Theory of Moral Sentiments*, which emphasised benevolence. Nor is he or she appeased to learn that in *The Wealth of Nations* itself, a few sentences before the notorious ones just quoted, Smith stressed how much man was a social animal and has almost constant occasion for the help of his brethren "While a human being's whole life is scarce sufficient to gain the friendship of a few persons, in civilised society he stands at all times in need of the co-operation and assistance of great multitudes. It is for this reason that he has to enlist their self love in his favour and cannot rely on their benevolence alone."

This self love will be effective only if certain background conditions are fulfilled. There has to be a legal system and a political order which enforce contracts, protect property rights, and provide for limited liability or the equivalent. In other words, there is no private property without good government. Until the disillusioning experience of post-Communist countries, such background considerations were regarded by many modern economists as too obvious or insufficiently mathematical to be worth discussing. Their neglect has made it all too easy for former Communist bosses to flip over to being Mafia-style capitalists instead.

But it is not the incompleteness of invisible hand statements which worries moralists, but their apparent reliance on the greed motive for the successful workings of an advanced civilisation. (A generation before Adam Smith a similar shock was supplied by Bernard Mandeville's *Fable of the Bees*, which suggested that the vices of the few were essential for the prosperity of the many.) The two most common reactions are either to reject Smith's doctrine as outrageous or to accept it in a cynical spirit and say that Smith understood that the world was a jungle and that the animal with the sharpest teeth would inevitably win (which was not what he thought at all).

A Rule Utilitarian Approach

There is, however, a third reaction which involves a little formal philosophy, although nothing more advanced than can be found in John Stuart Mill. This is to explain both the strength and limitations of the invisible hand doctrine in terms of a system of utilitarian morality. By utilitarianism I simply mean the view that actions are to be judged by their consequences for the welfare of other people. I do not have to argue whether utilitarianism can provide a complete system or whether it should be constrained by other ideas, such as those of Rawls which I discuss in Chapter Four. It is sufficient to say that public activities, whether in politics or business, are normally judged by utilitarian criteria; and it is difficult to see how this could be otherwise in a complex society.

Mill faced up to the problem of how to fit conventional moral rules such as, "Don't tell lies", or, "Keep promises", into utilitarian morality. He argued that we do not have the knowledge to assess directly on each separate occasion the effects of our actions on other human beings. What he called "the *prima facie* rules of common sense morality" arose from the common experience of mankind. The welfare of others will usually be better promoted by observing these rules rather than by trying to work out from first principles the effects of our behaviour on others on each separate occasion.

The invisible hand doctrine is one of the more surprising prima facie rules to have been suggested. Surprising because of its apparently cynical flavour. For it does suggest that we will often do others more good if we behave as if we are following our self-interest than by pursuing more obviously altruistic purposes.

Prima facie rules of acceptable behaviour are by definition subject to exception and qualification. There will always be difficult cases in personal life. which require reflection on basics There will always be exceptional cases in which accepted rules should be overridden. So the maxims of Adam Smith do not enable businessmen to escape moral reflection – and were not intended to do so. The absence of laws or conventions prohibiting the dumping of poisonous lead would not excuse indiscriminate dumping. Nor do they excuse the sale of landmines to unscrupulous users.

In general, the closer to hand are the effects of business conduct the easier it is to know when to make exceptions to the invisible hand doctrine. A takeover tycoon who shows an old retainer the door is a scoundrel and should not be excused by any market economist. The self-interest maxim comes in when we deal with remoter consequences. A business executive does not have the *knowledge* to estimate the remoter consequences of supposedly patriotic deviations from commercial self-interest such as buying British when the overseas product gives better value. Nor is such knowledge available to MPs, officials or even academic economists. A manufacturer who keeps open uneconomic enterprises to provide jobs is not necessarily promoting even the longer run interests of his immediate workforce. This is apart from the fact that, if he persists, he is likely to be taken over or abruptly closed down by successors, who may make the changes in a far more brutal way.

Information Requirements

An economic system has at least five functions. They are to:

1. co-ordinate the activity of millions of individuals, households and firms;

2. obtain information about people's desires, tastes and preferences;

3. decide which productive techniques to use;

4. promote new ideas, tastes and activities which people would not have thought of without entrepreneurial initiative;

5. create incentives for people to act on such information.

Only the fifth, incentive, function of markets could be abandoned in a community of saints. The others would still be required for the saints to know how best to serve their fellows. They might still be well advised to behave *as if* they were concerned with their own worldly well-being in order to create the market signals by which they could best serve others.

We know that the search for profit does not apply to large sections of activity. Institutions concerned with health and education are usually non profit-making even when their services are sold for cash. A distinguished musician or surgeon will often have a strong sense of vocation and not just play or operate for the money. A doctor or teacher should have some responsibility to his patient or pupil over and above the search for fees. Here market rates of pay have their effects at the margin. They bring in the less dedicated who might have chosen a different field of endeavour; and they affect even the dedicated in their choice at the margin between work and leisure, or choice of profession. A hospital management need not be interested in profit maximisation, but at least it should be interested in minimising costs. So condemnation of the internal market without examination is merely childish.

It is, however, time to query the pious belief that professional values are invariably superior to commercial ones. Professional bodies have their own inherent deficiencies. If left to themselves they often try to keep out new people and ideas and enforce restrictive practices. Many academics are opera lovers.

Have they forgotten the professional guild of the Meistersingers of Nuremburg, which tried to keep out new influences and new types of song and verse from their guild? It was no free market fanatic, but Paul Samuelson, the Democrat Nobel Prize winning economist, who long ago said that he preferred good clean money to bad dirty power.

Business Culture

But let us descend to a lower level of abstraction. Part of the Communitarian critique arises from an absurd idea of how a profit-seeking concern seeks to promote shareholder value. When I write an article for the Financial Times, the editor does not ask whether the article will increase the value of the Pearson equity. But he does know that, if the paper does not eventually make a return on its assets comparable to that of alternative investments, there is going to be trouble. As indeed there should be.

It is worth looking at the origin of the most criticised business attitudes, such as an exaggerated emphasis on the bottom line. They arise not from profit seeking or individualism as such, but from the separation of ownership from control. Modern economists have recognised something called the principal agent problem. How do we make sure that appointed managers do in fact act as trustees for the ultimate owners and do not squander the resources for their own aggrandisement or alternatively to lead a quiet life? The problem affects state property as well as private corporations. It still arises for enterprises owned by their own workers or by local communities.

It was because of frequent abuses of managerial power that the takeover culture developed. On the Continent, and especially in Germany, this same function is performed for large enterprises by banks via the business establishment. It is far from obvious that a closed network is a better method of control than open bids for stock ownership. Admiration for German corporate culture is mostly found in English-speaking countries.

Many of the tensions would be eased if there were a move to smaller units where the managers were also the proprietors. Ownership and control are combined in the German *Mittelstand* or in the flourishing medium sized Italian companies which are responsible for most of the real economic miracles in that country.

A manager who is merely a trustee for shareholders has to make his decisions in two halves. First, he has to earn as much as he can for the stockholders. Then he has to apportion the resulting earnings in a way which he believes the owners will approve. No wonder most top executives take the easy way out by some ploughing back, some dividend distribution and some token contribution, such as 1 per cent of profits, to good causes. How much easier it is for an owner of a ceramics factory in the Italian Veneto to make all his decisions in one go; and, if he has a good year, to send an immediate cheque to a local musical society or to help the renovation of a Palladian villa. It is his affair and there is no conflict between profit seeking and civic values.

The issue was brought home to me when, at a conference, I met a small American manufacturer whose main motive in life was to run a furniture factory profitable enough to give work to the disabled, who were paid something like normal wages. If he had been a mere manager, the shareholders could reasonably have demanded that he maximised his return on assets. As the owners, they could then decide what they wanted to do with the resulting profits, which might include providing work for the disabled at subsidised rates. But when the owner and the manager are the same person all these stages can be collapsed into one. It remains true that such an entrepreneur still does his best for the disabled or any other good cause by buying in the cheapest market and selling in the dearest.

The trend away from corporate dinosaurs towards smaller service companies which make separate contracts with individual purchasers could eventually lead to a much more dispersed pattern of economic decisions and a more personal form of individualism. But let us not pretend that everyone is going to like it. Salaried employees who are suddenly told to fend for themselves as consultants or suppliers of specialist services often find the process a shock – no matter how many books they have read or written decrying bureaucratic corporate management.

The True Bottom Line

It is not difficult to summarise the economic argument. A stakeholder or communitarian would like to see social and ethical objectives pursued directly by corporations in addition to, or instead of, the search for profit. Market liberals prefer to provide for these objectives in the background conditions and rules which constrain the search for profit. In many particular cases two reasonable members of both schools might agree. But the market liberal will always worry that the stakeholder arrogates to business leaders the role of shaping society for which they are ill suited; and that they would serve us as well as themselves better if they stuck to specific and limited objectives and did not take on the role of Moses and the minor prophets as well.

The debate will not be decided by evidence or formal reasoning alone. To communitarians selfishness is the most hideous of sins, and sometimes the only one. An individualist-liberal does not celebrate selfishness; but he believes that there can be worse sins, such as the sacrifice of individual human beings for the sake of some abstract doctrine or religious or other belief. If I may quote Holmes again:

> Communitarian anti-liberals suggest that, once people overcome their self-interest, they necessarily act in an admirable and public spirited way; but these leave out of account the prominent place of selfless cruelty in human affairs. It is much easier to be cruel in the course of acting in the cause of others than while acting for one's own thing. Those who have homosexuals shot in the name of the Islamic revolution cannot be accused of anti-social individualism or base self interest.

My own conviction is that people in the grip of greed often do much less harm than people in the grip of self-righteousness, especially when that righteousness is harnessed to the supposed needs of a collectivity or given some theological or metaphysical justification.

Appendix on Methodological Individualism

One kind of individualism which creates much heat is methodological individualism. This is the desire to ground social science in the behaviour and/or motivations of individual human beings. Neo-classical economic theory is based on this approach – although you would not guess so from the short-term forecaster in front of a screen who provides the public image of an economist. Most sociologists are hostile to methodological individualism; and indeed many economists write books denouncing the individualist foundations of their own subject.

Methodological individualism is itself a branch of a reductionism, which seeks to ground explanation in the most basic units. But why stop at individual human beings? Why not try to reduce motivation to biology, biology to chemistry, and chemistry in its turn to sub-atomic physics? Freud, for instance, started off hoping that his analysis could be reduced in the end to biochemistry; and the inability to make this translation has counted against the scientific status of psychoanalysis. Nevertheless, the test of success in the social sciences is prediction or explanation. It is better to have a more successful explanation of business cycles, which starts with mere statistical regularities, than one which is well grounded in hypotheses about individual behaviour, but which tells us very little we did not know already.

Purely methodological individualism ought to be neutral in relation to morals and politics. It is a matter of finding from experience the approach which yields the most fruitful hypotheses in a particular context.

There is, however, one reason why a social scientist might want to start from the individual human being rather than the group to which he or she belongs, or than the quarks of which he or she is composed. This is that the social scientist has an *advantage* over the physical scientist or the zoologist in being able to take into account motivations and intentions. And these exist at the level of the individual. It is odd to have to labour this point to Christian philosophers who place so much emphasis on free will and responsibility.

References

Boaz, David (1993). *Libertarianism*. Free Press.

Brittan, S., (1985). Wincott Memorial Lecture, 1985. Reprinted as Chapter 2 of *Capitalism with a Human Face*, London: Edward Elgar, 1995; paperback edition, Fontana, 1996.

Dawkins, R., (1989). *The Selfish Gene*. Revised edition, Oxford: University Press.

Etzioni, Amital, (1993). *The Spirit of Community*. New York: Crown Publishers.

Holmes, Stephen (1993). *The Anatomy of Anti-Liberalism*. Harvard: University Press.

McIntyre, Alasdair (1985). *After Virtue*. London: Duckworth, 2nd edition.

Macpherson, C. B., (1962). *The Political Theory of Possessive Individualism*, Oxford: University Press.

Mill, J. S., (1861). *Utilitarianism*. Modern edition, London: J M Dent (1948).

Mulhall, S., and Swift, A., (1997). *Liberals and Communitarians*, 2nd edition, Oxford: Blackwell.

Phillips, Melanie (1998). Unpublished paper delivered at the conference of the Royal Institute of Philosophy in September 1997, to be published in J Haldane (ed), *Philosophy and Public Affairs*, Cambridge: University Press.

Rawls, John (1972). *A Theory of Justice*. Oxford: University Press.

Samuelson, Paul (1962). *Problems of the American Economy*. London: University of London Athlone Press.

Smith, Adam (1759). *The Theory of Moral Sentiments*. Modern edition, Indianapolis: Liberty Classics (1982).

Smith, Adam (1776). *The Wealth of Nations*. Modern edition, Indianapolis: Liberty Classics (1981).

Chapter Two
Making Common Cause*

How liberals differ and what they ought to agree on

One of Gladstone's Chancellors of the Exchequer, Sir William Harcourt, achieved fame with just one remark: "We are all socialists now". Little did he realise how many British and American academics would – more than a century later – be claiming instead all to be liberals, admittedly with a small l. The label has come to cover a great many different kinds of liberalism, which are hardly on speaking terms with each other. These distinctions emerge all too clearly from two recent books.

The first is a conference volume on *The Liberal Political Tradition* edited by James Meadowcroft. The emphasis here is on the expanding role of government in securing citizen welfare. Global capitalism is seen by many of the contributors as an enemy of reform. One of the essays even entertains the idea that the GATT trade agreements are chiefly effective in justifying or sustaining the interest of the privileged nations of the world – overlooking how the emerging countries fought for the latest agreement in the teeth of entrenched Western protectionism. Amidst all these fashionable concerns, traditional liberal fears about the tyranny of a majority are brushed aside.

The second volume self-consciously follows in the wake of John Locke, the English philosopher who believed that governments existed to protect the legitimate rights of life, liberty and property and should be overthrown when they did not do so. Indeed, the essays are sponsored by an American body known as the Locke Institute, and the series in which they appear is entitled The Shaftesbury Papers after John Locke's political patron. The book is meant to set out the modern case for a minimal or nightwatchman state confined to providing security. These authors undoubtedly regard themselves as being in the liberal tradition. In fact Norman Barry's contribution is entitled "Classical Liberalism in the Age of Post-Communism". The Shaftesbury authors see the chief threat to liberty as state economic intervention, high public expenditure and the redistributive activities of the welfare state. Although not all the authors come entirely clean on the subject, the alleviation of poverty is seen largely as a matter of voluntary insurance or private benevolence with, at most, a very minimal state redistribution to those not

*Reprinted from *Times Literary Supplement*, 20 September 1996.

so covered – and some of the authors would regard even this concession as rank heresy.

Discussions of liberalism are hampered by a confused mass of overlapping terminology. Meadowcroft's interventionist liberals were known at the beginning of this century as New Liberals; today they are often called left liberals, but sometimes "liberals in the American sense". Those in the Locke tradition may be called "liberals in the European sense" or (by their opponents) ultra-liberals, supporters of Anglo-Saxon capitalism, libertarians, or (very misleadingly) the New Right. To avoid becoming bogged down in arguments about words, it might be useful to follow Ralf Dahrendorf's suggestion and call the original liberals of the early nineteenth century classical liberals, the more interventionist ones social liberals (they can hardly complain as they love the word social) and the modern exponents of a limited state, neo-liberals. The latter, of course, regard themselves as the heirs to classical liberalism.

There is a temptation to treat the two books separately as expressions of highly conflicting beliefs, not even emanating from the same academic subject area. But we should pause before doing so. Both books claims to be about liberalism and both make reference to common founding fathers, such as Locke, Hume, Montesqieu, Bentham and Mill. The two volumes even come from the same publisher, although from divisions which do not seem to talk to one another.

What should one conclude from the chasm between these works? It would be extremely easy to see liberalism as a historical movement whose time has passed. It was conceived as a drive in favour of personal freedom against despotism, censorship and irresponsible government. When public spending was largely either on armies or on the provision of sinecures for favourites, all liberals could unite under slogans such as Peace, Retrenchment and Reform. When the archetypal example of economic intervention was the Corn Laws, which raised the price of bread, there was no difficulty in a Manchester manufacturer and a working class radical making common cause against them.

But now that so much intervention is ostensibly designed to help the poor or to blunt the blows sometimes inflicted by economic forces, a split seems unavoidable. Those who worry mainly about preserving economic freedom tend to become a conservative sub-group, while those interested not only in the condition of the people but also in causes such as anti-censorship or open government find themselves on the left. They then become indistinguishable from social democrats or moderate non-Marxist socialists, once the latter abandon their belief in wholesale nationalisation. Indeed, many social liberals would regard Tony Blair's Labour Party as far too friendly to market capitalism.

The linguistic burial of liberalism would thus be an easy road to take. Political labels are matters of convenience and do not have essential meanings. The case for the linguistic burial of liberalism is strengthened by the dwindling of political parties called Liberal. (The small parties which still retain the name are essentially social democrat groups and are not taken seriously by any of the rival academic writers.) As Rodney Barker reminds us in his contribution to *The Liberal Tradition*:

> While the history of conservatism is mapped along . . . contours etched by the work of the Thatcher government in the United Kingdom, and the development of nationalism in the creation of Slovakia, Croatia and the new states of the former Soviet Union, the history of liberalism is marked by the publication of John Rawls's *A Theory of Justice*, Robert Nozick's *Anarchy, State and Utopia*, or the debates in academic journals.

Nevertheless, the separation of the two kinds of liberalism in the world of politics impoverishes them both; and so even does their separation in the world of academic disputation. It is, therefore, still worth looking for ideas which both sides ought to be able to share. Social liberalism is impoverished when its adherents fail to see that freedom to spend one's own income in one's own way – above all in sensitive areas such as health and education – is an essential part of freedom. So too is freedom to start a business or to move money across frontiers. But neo-liberal practice and thought are impoverished when there is too great a concentration on ownership, earning and spending, and when matters such as open government or the rights of suspects against the police are overlooked. The distortion reaches ridiculous levels when neo-liberal economists publish league tables of so-called economic freedom in which South East Asian dictatorships come out on top, high above the more tolerant societies of Western Europe. Thus some neo-liberals leave themselves wide open to Anthony Arblaster's charge in the Meadowcroft book that:

> While much Western advice and support has been made available to assist and speed up the conversion of the state socialist economies into full blown capitalist ones . . . nothing like the same effort has been put into facilitating the transition from authoritarianism to democracy . . . Imagine the chorus of condemnation that would have greeted Boris Yeltsin's ruthless suppression of parliamentary resistance in Moscow in 1993 or his cruel war against Chechenya in 1994–95 if he had happened to be a Communist president of the Soviet Union rather than the ex-Communist president of post-Communist Russia.

Any reunification of liberalism today would have to be primarily in the world of ideas. The task is not made easier by the desire of the two kinds of writers to remain as far apart as possible. Several writers in *The Liberal Political Tradition* endeavour to expel from modern liberalism neo-liberal economists such as Hayek and Friedman. Their concentration on these two near-household names does not suggest a first-hand acquaintance with the market liberal case. Have they even heard of other neo-liberal economists such as James Buchanan, who is the real inspirer of the Shaftesbury Papers?

The one person who contributes to both volumes is Norman Barry, himself a neo-liberal. But, so far from wanting to break down barriers, he is more concerned to reinforce them. His main point is that today's neo-liberals, who start from the basis of academic economics, are thoroughly suspicious of any sort of politics. Indeed, they debate among themselves the relative virtues of some form of anarcho-capitalism versus the minimal state.

At this point it is instructive to look back at the Liberal statesman who dominated British politics for several decades, namely W E Gladstone. It did not occur to that great man to debate the existence of the state or to denigrate the role of politics. He was far too busy with matters such as a free trade treaty with France, the rights of Jews to take their seats in parliament and the redress of Irish grievances. In practice, he believed in a highly limited sphere for political activity, which was more useful than a vain attempt to get rid of it altogether.

Yet, despite their unashamedly ivory tower orientation, the Shaftesbury writers are a good deal more interesting than the Meadowcroft ones. They are engaged in an attempt to work out rigorously the purposes for which rational human beings deliberating together would surrender some of their rights to government, and how government can then be prevented from exceeding its proper remit. One root of their thinking lies in the fathers of the American Constitution, such as Jefferson, Hamilton and, above all, Madison, whose deliberations were published in the Federalist Papers. Another root lies in modern welfare economics.

As political economists they differ from some of their colleagues in not indulging in mathematics for its own sake, although they are willing to do so occasionally (especially in diagrammatic form) when they think it really helps. A more substantial difference from their mainstream colleagues is that they are unwilling to trade the reduction of one person's welfare against an improvement in another's. (To put it in jargon, they take seriously the Pareto criterion for an improvement.) They also differ from the best known exponent of contractarian reasoning, the philosopher John Rawls, in insisting that they should start from endowments which people actually have, rather than from hypothetical endowments which they would grant each other in a state of ignorance.

Their problem, however, is the lack of a classical liberal theory of legitimate property rights. John Locke's idea that they derived from something in which a person had mixed his labour was inadequate even in the seventeenth century. Moreover, in Locke's original position it was also important that, after people had appropriated property (in practice land), there should be good and enough left over – a qualification which neither he nor his successors ever fully developed. Barry, to his credit, is aware of this lacuna.

As a result, today's neo-liberals are apt to clutch at any straw, such as Kirzner's idea that the rewards of entrepreneurship legitimately belong to the entrepreneur. Maybe. But such rewards fail to account for a very large proportion of today's property holdings. In my view there is no escape from some hypothetical contract among disinterested people – of which the results may be a good deal less egalitarian than Rawls would like.

If one looks hard enough, there are a few pointers in these two books to some potential common ground between the two liberalisms. Barry sees some hope in the ideas of civic society, dear to the heart of the Czech President Vaclav Havel, which emphasises voluntary groups which are neither state organs nor profit-making businesses. In his contribution to the Shaftesbury Papers (but unfortunately only in a footnote), De Jasay denounces the strain of vulgarised anti-collectivist discourse which overlooks that civil society can function in many spheres as well as in and through the market.

There are perplexities in the civic route. Many of the most highly valued communal groups have their oppressive conformist side, a paradox never explored better than in Wagner's *Meistersingers of Nuremburg*. Moreover, whatever their other virtues, highly developed social and professional networks provide a fertile soil for the interest group influences which so pervert the modern state and, incidentally, reduce their growth potential.

There are firmer areas of common ground. If one tries to demarcate a body of belief, it is often useful to ask what its adherents are against. Two traditional liberal beliefs which should surely be common threads among their present-day successors is suspicion of nationalism and the slogan "Democracy is not enough". To any kind of liberal a mere majority vote (let alone a plurality) does not make oppressive conduct permissible. Democracy is a convenient decision rule for changing governments, without the use of force, and for voting in assemblies. But it cannot justify an unjust war or the infliction of cruel and unusual punishments. It can neither justify the expropriation of people's property nor the rolling back of those social services which people have come to take for granted and are seen as property rights.

Indeed, the best reasons for neo-liberals to keep their distance from conservatism can be found in Hayek's *Constitution of Liberty*, which appeared in 1960, in the Appendix entitled "Why I am Not a Conservative". One of his reasons – that the Macmillan Conservatives of the time accepted too much of the over-extended state – would have been hastily dismissed by social liberals as mere reaction. But his other reasons could not be so treated. "The conservative," he remarks, "does not object to coercion or arbitrary power so long as it is used for what he regards as the right purposes . . . If the government is in the hands of decent men it ought not to be too much restricted by rigid rules. The typical conservative is indeed usually a man of very strong moral convictions but he has no political principles which enable him to work with people whose moral values differ from his own."

Hayek also remarks that the conservative's distrust of the new and strange is clearly connected with his proneness to strident nationalism. But for a liberal it is not a real argument to say that an idea is un-American, un-British or un-German. Moreover, the nationalistic bias provides a bridge to collectivism. To think of "our" industry or resources is only a short way from demanding that they be directed in the national interest.

Nothing is going to make a social liberal love capitalism or a present-day follower of John Locke dance a jig at the foot of the Welfare State. But a realisation that they can agree on some human rights and on the limitations of both democracy and nationalism might just make them see that the beliefs which they ought to have in common are at least as important as those which divide them. For, if liberals do not come together, the grim picture we have ahead of us is of politicians still trying to enact their slightest whim under the sacred name of a democratic mandate, and of these same politicians tacitly encouraging the yobs who use everything from football matches to minor agricultural disputes to stir up hatred against fellow human beings in neighbouring countries.

A book which I often use to cheer myself up is entitled *The Liberal Tradition from Fox to Keynes*, edited by Alan Bullock and Maurice Shock, and published in 1956, which consists of extracts from classic Liberal texts. The critic can have some fun contrasting the part near the end entitled "The End of Laissez-Faire", consisting of passages from Keynes and Beveridge, with earlier sections by the classical political economists commending economic individualism. But much the greater part of the book is taken up with matters on which both sorts of liberals should be able to agree. There are eloquent addresses on civil liberties by Charles James Fox and also his classic speeches in opposition to the war against Revolutionary France. There is Byron on freedom as well as Adam Smith on free trade, together with John Stuart Mill on representative government. There are sections on popular education, religious liberty, Irish freedom and, above all, Mill's classic statement of the case for personal freedom in actions where others are not adversely affected.

But perhaps the litmus test of whether the reader is in any sense a liberal or not is his reaction to some of Gladstone's foreign policy speeches. As early as 1850, when he had not yet completed his journey from Peelite Toryism, Gladstone intervened in the Don Pacifico debate to denounce the idea that a Foreign Secretary should be mainly concerned with British aggrandisement, and proclaimed that his main business should be to be a force for peace in the concert of Europe: "I think it to be the very first of all his duties studiously to observe, and to exalt in honour among mankind, that great code of principles which is termed the law of nations."

In a much later passage, taken from the late 1870s, around the time of the Midlothian Campaign, he reminded his listeners that

> the sanctity of life in the hill villages of Afghanistan among the winter snows, is as inviolable in the eye of almighty God as can be your own . . . that the law of mutual love is not limited by the shores of this island, is not limited by the boundaries of Christian civilisation; that it passes over the whole surface of the earth, and embraces the meanest along with the greatest in its unmeasured scope.

By all means smile at the oratory. But anyone who sneers at the underlying message is not a liberal in any sense of that word worth preserving.

References

Meadowcroft, J., (ed), (1996). *The Liberal Political Tradition: Contemporary Reappraisals*. Cheltenham: Edward Elgar.

Rowley, C. K., (1996). *The Political Economy of the Minimal State*. Cheltenham: Edward Elgar.

Chapter Three
Redistributive Market Liberalism*

J S Mill

When your Trustees kindly asked me to give the John Stuart Mill Lecture they were knocking against an open door. For Mill has always been, if not exactly my hero, my intellectual and political beacon. If any single book marks out the defining features of Western civilisation, as distinct from its mere technical accomplishments, it is Mill's *On Liberty*, a work which magnificently survives generations of nit-picking criticism.

Mill wrote many other major treatises on political philosophy, logic, economics and constitutional reform, many of which could still form the agenda of contemporary discussion. And his whole life was a protest against mindless conformity – but never to the point of overthrowing rationality or the decencies of personal behaviour.

Of course, Mill had his faults. He had an unattractive priggishness, expressed for instance in his dislike of the self-interest motive as other than a necessary and perhaps temporary evil. Moreover, his tortuous and reluctant condemnation of the monopolistic and coercive activities of trade unions – however understandable in the social conditions of the mid-nineteenth century – set an unfortunate precedent for later intellectuals anxious to maintain their left-wing credentials.

I would not, however, condemn Mill because he was simultaneously attracted by contrasting sets of ideas: Benthamite individualism and the Romantic movement; democracy and elitism; co-operation and competition; liberty and fraternity. Such strictures are misguided. These concepts are not logical contradictories, but different ideals. And it is perfectly realistic to want to combine as much as possible of any pair. In the unlovely jargon of modern economics, this would be called improving the trade-offs. But, jargon aside, it is an eminently sensible endeavour.

In a paper for a Royal Institute of Philosophy conference in St Andrews (reprinted as Chapter 1 of this book) I argued that individualism has suffered from being wrongly confused with selfishness; and that communitarians are in

* The John Stuart Mill Lecture, delivered at the National Liberal Club, November 1997. Published together with other material in *Towards a Humane Individualism*, John Stuart Mill Institute, 1 Whitehall Place, London SW1A 2HE.

danger of making a fetish of groups, over and above the individuals of which they are composed. In this lecture. I shall be discussing more positively the political economy of liberalism with a small "l"

Capital "L" Liberalism

It would be other-worldly for me to continue further without noting that the John Stuart Mill Institute – while admirably open to people of all parties and of none – is supported particularly strongly by those who have been and are active in politics as "Liberals with a capital L"; and it is no accident that we are meeting in the National Liberal Club. I have to confess that, although I have been writing and speaking for many years on liberalism, with that famous small "l", this is the first time that I have addressed a large group of Liberals with a capital "L".

Mill was of course a liberal in both senses. He even sat, reluctantly, in Parliament for one term (1865–1868). But he wore his capital letter allegiance lightly. Not only did he abjure anything like "pavement politics". He made it a condition of standing that he would concentrate on national issues and refuse to represent the special interests of his constituents. Today he would be condemned as "off message".

Whatever I may think of the particular drift of the Liberal policies, I cannot but pay tribute to the dedication of generations of people who have worked against seemingly hopeless odds to prevent a complete domination of politics by two political dinosaurs. A reward came in an unexpectedly large gain of seats for the Liberal Democrats in the 1997 election.

As a matter of realpolitik, continued co-operation with Tony Blair is essential. Without electoral reform, the 1997 result could prove yet another false dawn. But further along the road there is a parting of the ways. The Liberal Democrats could become the conscience of the left, allying themselves with some elements of Old Labour and pushing for more collective activity than New Labour is prepared to accept. This is a perfectly honourable path; and it could be combined with resistance to the more authoritarian instincts of New Labour. If that is what most active Liberals would like, they will not be put off by the shade of Gladstone, still less by commentators like myself.

There is however an alternative. It is that followed by the German Free Democrats, who have sometimes been allied with the Social Democrats and sometimes with the Christian Democrats, and are often in different coalitions in different Länder. It is the changes in their alliances which has preserved them as an independent fore. If British Liberal Democrats want to follow that course, it will mean occasionally talking to Conservatives and not being mesmerised by words, such as right wing, which derives from the placing of parties in the French Assembly after the 1789 Revolution.

Redistributive Market Liberalism – RML

These last few remarks are emphatically intended as a digression. Since Mill's time, academic theorists have been arguing about liberalism's characteristics as a body of political philosophy, without much reference to the changing platform of political Liberals with a capital L.

The gulf partly reflects the long domination of British public life by the Labour and Conservative parties under the first-past-the-post system. It has, however, the redeeming feature that the more armchair kind of liberal has been able to follow the argument wherever it leads, and can also try to convince opinion formers of all political parties and of none.

Even armchair liberalism has, however, been badly divided. On one side are the liberals in the American sense, who are sometimes called social liberals on this side of the Atlantic. They are keen on state intervention, sceptical of market capitalism and are optimistic about collective action. On the other side are the classical market or individualist liberals, who emphasise personal choice, property rights and competitive markets.

Words do not have essential meanings; and there is no point in fighting about which side has the better claim to the name liberal. But, as I have argued previously, the divorce between these two schools of thought has impoverished both sides.

As some of you will know – or fear – my sympathies are with the classical liberals. But I cannot identify completely with their present spokesmen. The core classical liberal belief, as far as I am concerned, is Mill's statement in *On Liberty*:

> The sole end for which mankind are warranted, individually or collectively, in interfering with the liberty of action of any of their number is self protection . . . His own good, either physical or moral, is not a sufficient warrant.

The principle is often called negative freedom in political philosophy and non-paternalism in economics. Specific economic systems, such as competitive market capitalism, are merely means for extending such choices as far as possible.

Unfortunately, some contemporary economic intellectuals have a different emphasis. They agree upon non-paternalism, but they also take the prevailing distribution of wealth and income as sacrosanct and regard the alleviation of poverty mainly as a matter of voluntary insurance or private benevolence. I do not think these beliefs have anything to do with crypto-Toryism – even Margaret Thatcher always kept such ideas at arm's length. Their extremism largely reflects the fact that classical liberalism has become very much an academic movement in a way it was not in its heyday under Cobden and Gladstone.

There is, of course, nothing inherently right about the pattern of rewards produced by the combination of inheritance and the market. But the way to introduce correctives is not to impose vague stakeholder responsibilities on business or to preach against self-interest. It is to devise a framework of rules – including, if necessary, redistributive taxation and transfers – by which a market economy can be induced to serve broader objectives. Adair Turner, the director general of the Confederation of British Industry, has very helpfully invented a name for this modified set of classical beliefs. This is Redistributive Market Liberalism or "RML". Until somebody comes out with something more scintillating, I propose to borrow the initials RML to describe my own beliefs. Of course, Turner is in no way responsible for the way they are developed here.

Ladder and Safety Net

Mill himself wrote that the laws of production were as unalterable as those of physics, but the laws of distribution reflected institutions which we are at liberty to change. In modern terms, this amounts to saying that we can have many of the benefits of a market economy while redistributing the cash counters with which people play the market game.

Some economists have sneered at Mill's distinction on the grounds that redistribution will inevitably affect the pattern of production and prices, and even the technologies which it pays to adopt. But neither Mill nor his modern successors have claimed that the exact pattern of production will remain unchanged – this would be a foolish thing to try to conserve. What they are saying is that the benefits of the market system, such as its ability to use decentralised knowledge and respond to changing consumer requirements, do not depend on maintaining the original distribution of income.

Despite Mill's warning, it is unfortunately necessary to spell out that sensible redistribution may involve a minimum income, but it does not mean minimum wages or any other kind of interference with competitive wage and price setting. The main result of such intervention is to price people out of work, as has occurred to a large extent on the continent of Europe. We should seek instead changes in the rules of the game – for instance in property and inheritance laws, and also in transfers through taxes and benefits. Keynes once said that there was more scope for redistribution through fiscal policy than through direct interference with prices and wages, although there was not unlimited scope along either route.

Why did Keynes say that that there was not unlimited scope even through taxes and transfers? Redistribution is bounded by two constraints: how much citizens ought or desire to redistribute; and how far they can go without dangerously impairing incentives, that is killing the goose which lays the golden egg.

The one plausible method of examining how much we ought to redistribute is known as contractarianism. This is a modern adaptation of an idea going back to John Locke and which has been developed in our own day by, among others, the American philosopher John Rawls. He suggests a thought experiment: a veil of ignorance in which we ask ourselves what arrangements we would support if we did not know our own place in the hierarchy – whether we were going to be millionaires or paupers or anywhere in between. But in contrast to Rawls, I believe that such a thought experiment is most likely to lead to what Winston Churchill called "the ladder and the safety net". That is a ladder of opportunity for all and a minimum below which no one can fall. How high the safety net should be is inherently a subjective matter on which people of goodwill will disagree. Complete equality exists only in the graveyard. (The subject is discussed in more detail in the next chapter)

Just as difficult a question as how much we ought to redistribute is how much we safely can. It is counter-productive to push redistribution to a point where it reduces economic performance so much that the beneficiaries fail to gain, or even lose. The traditional analysis is in terms of incentives in a closed economy. Beyond a certain point, the combined effect of taxes and benefits is to reduce hours worked and also the proportion of the population seeking employment at any given real wage. This limit depends not only on the amount of redistribution, but just as much on the exact details of the tax and benefit system. Today the greater threat is not internal but external tax exile. Capital is highly mobile in the medium term. Owners both of capital and of scarce skills will either pass on any excess tax burden or move to where they can earn the international rate of return.

The moral is not that we should give up redistribution; rather, we should concentrate the tax burden on the less mobile elements. Of course, the least mobile factor of production is land. The case for land taxation has been made by many generations of political economists but has never been easy to implement. At the very least, if the present Government wants to make death duties effective instead of voluntary, it should – not before time – shift to a progressive accessions duty which would tax the size of the inheritance and not the capital sum bequeathed. Apart from that, the best bet might be to concentrate on taxing long-lived capital structures which embody a large element of land in their price – that is not plant and machinery but commercial buildings and domestic residences. Above all, we must avoid the temptation to bring back confiscatory marginal taxes on a higher incomes. It might make some people feel more self-righteous, but it would not help the poor.

Negative Income Tax and Basic Income

This is not the occasion for a thorough review of the tax and social security system. But, if we are to examine fundamentals, a little bit of detail is unavoidable. Conceptually, the simplest form of tax and transfer is a Negative, or Reverse, Income Tax (NIT). In such a system there is a break-even point above which you pay tax and below which you receive from the state – in other words, other citizens. As your original income rises, you receive less and less benefit, and eventually you cross over into the zone of positive taxpaying.

The key numbers are the minimum benefit for those without other income and the rate at which this benefit tapers off as original income rises. Basic Income (BI) is a form of Negative Income Tax in which there is a single implicit marginal rate which applies both to benefit withdrawal and to tax itself. If there is, say, a 50 per cent tax rate, benefit falls off by 50p for each pound by which original income rises.

The tax system inherited by the Blair Government did indeed attempt, however imperfectly, to provide a top-up for those without sufficient resources. Some of the advantages of both Negative Income Tax and Basic Income are administrative and psychological. Recipients are dealt with by the tax authorities rather than the social security inspectors. But do not carry this too far. If the system is to cater for the varying needs of different sized families, one-parent families and individual hardship not reducible to legislative formulae, it will always be complicated.

There are, however, other differences. A pure tax and transfer system eliminates any kind of work test. Deficiency of income is enough. To my mind, this is an advantage in helping people to avoid being complete wage slaves and in facilitating an opt-out of the economic struggle for those willing to live on modest means. But, alas, public opinion is not yet ready to make such transfers to those to whom it regards as workshy. An NIT or BI would today have to include a willing-to-work test, which might ultimately be expanded to include voluntary work or activity in the arts or sports.

Another bone of contention is that, if there is a single rate for both benefit withdrawal and for income tax, there will be a large spillover of benefits quite high up the income scale, as I have discussed in an earlier work. For a given net cost, either the basic benefit is lower or the marginal tax rate is higher throughout the income scale. For that reason I would for the moment favour a Negative Income Tax rather than a pure Basic Income: in other words, a withdrawal rate for benefits steeper than the basic rate of income tax. If we are to concentrate resources on those who need them most, some element of surtax on lower incomes is inevitable.

It does not, however, have to be as steep as it is. Even after the Fowler reforms of the mid-1980s, the combination of Housing Benefit and Family Credit (the income top-up-scheme), which are both withdrawn simultaneously as income rose, leading to very high withdrawal rates. A priority in any reform, should be to transfer as much as possible of Housing Benefit to Family Credit (now re-christened Working Families Tax Credit), and to leave Housing Benefits as a residual for some inner city areas where the market price of basic accommodation looks like being unaffordably high for the foreseeable future.

Welfare to Work

There is an obvious similarity between the aims of Negative Income Tax and those of Labour's Welfare to Work drive. The analogy will be closer when the government shifts the payment of benefits from the social security to the tax system, as under the US Earned Income Tax Credit. The big difference is between benefits and top-ups of all kinds and the Frank Field concept of compulsory insurance to make people less dependent on the Welfare State. May I suggest a King Solomon's judgment? The insurance approach should be used for pensions, and the tax and transfer one for citizens of working age.

A liberal, in the sense of a non-paternalist, will, however, clearly want to limit the extent of compulsion in retirement provision to the minimum required to provide a pension big enough not to need supplementation. People with larger incomes should make their own decisions about how far to pay for larger pensions to maintain their living standards in retirement. For citizens of working age, going the whole hog towards Basic Income would go some way to combat Frank Field's fears about the dependency culture. For then everyone would have a minimum income as of right; and the incentive to cheat would be no greater for benefit recipients than for normal income taxpayers today.

In 1997, Lord Desai made an estimate of the cost of a Basic Income of £50 per week to each adult, with more for those above 65. This would replace the Job Seekers' Allowance, Income Support, Family Credit and the basic state pension. (His estimates were made with the aid of Holly Sutherland's Polimod model.) He calculated that it would have cost an extra 12p on the basic rate of income tax, which would then have risen to 35 per cent (to which of course employee National Insurance contribution of 10 per cent, and probably also employer contribution of another 10 per cent, should be added). This is within the same ball park as the extra 15p on the basic income tax rate estimated by Steven Webb for a slightly different proposal, canvassed in a joint paper with myself.

Before throwing up your hands in horror, please remember that recipients would have the option of taking the basic income as a personal allowance against tax payments. This netting-out would mean that many people would actually hand over smaller sums to the state than they do today. There is a also a more fundamental point. An economic liberal should makes a sharp distinction between state services in kind and cash transfers. Services in kind, however worthy, reduce the income which citizens can spend at their discretion. Taken to extremes, they would leave us with nothing but pocket money to spend. Cash transfers do not reduce personal choice at all, but simply redistribute the counters with which that choice is exercised.

In exploring a Basic Income, which I do not immediately advocate, I am following Mill's example of being prepared to discuss ideas which are not yet practical in the present state of humanity but to whose realisation we should look forward.

Three sources of income

A large part of existing cash benefits do not represent a net transfer from higher to lower lifetime incomes. They represent instead a transfer among the same people between different phases of their lives. For instance, a family on median income will be a net tax payer when it starts out, a net beneficiary when there are dependent children, a net payer when the children grow up, and a net beneficiary again when pension age is reached. Among people of the same lifetime income, there are thus transfers between periods of high and low earnings.

Should a liberal, in the non-paternalist sense, advocate ending these vertical transfers and concentrating on transfers to families of low life-time income? Unfortunately, this is not very practical, however non-paternalist one wishes to be. Consider a person who is now unemployed or with low earnings, and receiving benefit. Neither that person, nor the government machine, has any idea whether he or she is suffering from a temporary misfortune and will in the end receive a high lifetime income, or whether the impoverished condition is more lasting. This same doubt will make it very difficult to borrow money to maintain living standards during the adverse period. So there is little alternative to going by weekly or, at most, yearly income at the particular time.

A much more difficult matter, hardly touched on by political philosophers, concerns the widespread desire for security. How far should we go in supporting people who are by no means near the bottom of the economic pile, but who have suffered severe shocks in a rapidly changing world? These range all the way from the traditional examples of skilled factory workers who have been made redundant by cheaper imports to the more topical cases of middle-ranking managers who now have so much anxiety about being made redundant. It is not sufficient to preach to people to put aside sums for a rainy day. Insurance markets can take care of specific contingencies, such as old age or, to a limited extent, sickness; but a trader in the derivatives market can hardly insure against his skills being in less demand in five years' time.

Yet once one advocates state-enforced transfers to middle income groups, any feasible scheme is bound to involve poorer taxpayers paying to the not-so-poor, which is difficult to justify morally or politically. Looking a good many years ahead, the furthest we can hope to go is towards a full Basic Income in which, as I already indicated, a certain amount of such spillover takes place automatically.

In the end, the best insurance against the exigencies of life would be a more widespread ownership of capital other than one's own house. Marx made quite the wrong criticism of private ownership of capital. The only thing wrong with investment or unearned income is that not enough of us have it.

Professor James Meade, the Nobel prize-winning economist who died in 1995, always struck me as being more nearly a reincarnation of Mill than any other contemporary political or economic thinker. In the last few years of his life, he envisaged a situation in which a typical citizen would have three sources of income: first, a wage or salary; secondly a basic income payment from the state; and, thirdly, some income from capital ownership, over and above the family home.

I know no magic way of bringing the third element about. It is possible for fiscal experts to think of all kinds of elaborate schemes, ranging from moderate annual capital levies to a series of budget surpluses to be used directly or indirectly for distributing capital all round. But I suspect that they will lack appeal. And, even if they do not deter overseas inward investment, they may deter the establishment of small businesses, which surely must play an important part in any property owning democracy.

Beyond this, it is a matter of looking for whatever opportunities come our way to encourage dispersed ownership. We missed a chance when privatisation shares were sold on the capital market rather than being handed over to all citizens on a *pro-rata* basis. We may have something to learn from the experience of the former Communist countries, some of which have issued very cheap vouchers to be used to purchase assets in state enterprises. In Russia it seems that many of these vouchers have been bought up at bargain prices by Mafia operators, but this may not be true nearly to the same extent in the Czech

Republic or Poland. Another example has been in Alaska where state oil revenues have been distributed as credits to all citizens.

Services in Kind

Although social security payments are the largest single part of the Welfare State, benefits in kind, mainly health and education, together amount to four-fifths as much. How should a non-paternalist regard them? Let me try to offer a few pointers.

If it were simply a matter of poor people not being able to afford medical treatment, cash transfers could take care of the problem. The difficulty with health is that needs for medical attention, however defined, vary enormously and unpredictably among people of comparable incomes. There can be medical catastrophes which would be a savage blow even to the chairman of a utility company or to a super businesswoman like Nicola Horlick.

Insurance cannot be a complete answer for all kinds of technical reasons, including the problem of moral hazard and also the ability of the medical profession, notorious in the USA, to bump up payments for medical treatment when insurance companies are meeting the bill. But a non-paternalist should not leave the matter there. Most people have to pay moderate sums for medical treatment in the course of a year, however healthy they are. The treatment for which they ask, or the drugs which they buy, are partly a matter of choice. The Health Service was founded on the principle of hard and fast need, ascertainable by experts, which is quite out-of-date today.

Why should not people pay for the first few hundred pounds of medical treatment, with perhaps some of the exemptions which apply for prescription charges today? State financial support is necessary for what are termed medical catastrophes. Maybe we should try compulsory insurance for in-between expenses such as routine operations or illnesses requiring heavy expenditure on drugs. Or, alternatively, or in addition, a shared payment between the patient and the state, as in some continental countries, might be considered.

Education is more difficult. The problem is that a large part of educational spending is for children – whom even John Stuart Mill did not regard as able to make their own decisions. If we were sure that parents always understood and would be willing to pay for the needs of their children, we would not need any state educational arrangement. Unfortunately, we cannot take this for granted. But, despite all the many disgraceful cases of ill-treatment and neglect, on balance parents are better judges of their children's needs than the Department of Education, local authorities or even school governing bodies.

> That the whole or any large part of the education of the people would be in state hands, I go as far as anyone in deprecating. All that has been said of the importance of individuality of character, and diversity of opinion and modes of conduct, involves as of the same unspeakable importance, diversity of education.
>
> A general state education is a mere contrivance for moulding people to be exactly like one another. An education established and controlled by the state should only exist, if it exists at all, as one among many competing experiments

carried on for the purpose of example and stimulus. The government might leave to parents to obtain the education where and how they pleased, and content itself with helping to pay the school fees of the poorer classes of children, and defraying the entire school expenses of those who have no-one else to pay for them.

These last sentences are not my own. Nor are they Margaret Thatcher's in an unguarded moment. They come from the last chapter of *On Liberty*.

It is a strength of the educational voucher proposal that it allows the state to enforce both minimum standards and minimum expenditure on education. But, within these limits, it allows parents a good deal of choice. If parents wish to top up their vouchers by spending their own money on extra lessons or musical tuition, or even skiing holidays, true liberals cannot object.

Some will rush to reply that poor families would be less able to make such top-ups. But we need to go slowly. For those who are really concerned with the needs of the less well off and are not just looking for debating points against parental choice, the remedy is at hand. It is to make the value of the voucher vary inversely with parental income, a course already advocated by some left-of-centre groups in the USA. In other words, give larger vouchers to the poor than to the rich. There is nothing very novel here. In the heyday of government grants for university students, middle class and better off parents had to make much larger parental contributions than poorer ones.

If we truly value personal choice, we should also think of giving more say to young people themselves. Followers of Mill's doctrines on freedom can hardly believe that children should be complete slaves of their parents or of their schools or colleges until some magic age such as 18 or 21. They should think instead of a gradual transition from infancy, when decisions have to be made by elders, to more advanced ages, when young people might have learned to participate in making more of their own choices.

In any case, the slogan that the government's priorities are "education, education and education" is superficial. It is based on a profound confusion between education and training. It is training about which governments really worry. And liberals ought to have a profound scepticism about the ability of governments or training boards to foresee the skills which are likely to be in demand in the future. Unfortunately, there is a good deal of evidence that official training programmes make little difference to job prospects.

Personally, I would scrap the whole bureaucratic training effort in return for cash grants or loans to young people, dependent only on their giving some proof that it has been spent on activities relevant to their future earnings capacity. I would define the latter very broadly to include backpacking around the world or helping in villages in poor or emerging countries. These are just as likely to provide the streetwise skills helpful to earning a living today as the large number of paper credentials now so much in vogue.

Conclusion

The policy suggestions just mentioned are not intended to provide a detailed blueprint. (The suggestions are filled out a little in Chapter Seven on the Welfare

State).They are merely a few pointers to how one could combine a resolute individualism and attachment to market principles with a redistribution of the counters with which the market game is played.

The hard collectivism of Communism has disintegrated. So has the vision of a planned democratic socialist society. But we are still threatened by softer and more seductive forms of collectivism. These have in common with their predecessors the delusion that the group is more important than the individuals of which it is composed. On the right this is seen in an outmoded devotion to the nation state and a hostility to the European Union which is always in danger of degenerating into a shrill chauvinism. On the left it embodies worship of an ill-defined community which, in practice, becomes a pervasive bossiness in matters ranging from intolerance of smoking to attempts to impose homework norms by central government.

The dividing lines today are at least as much on the freedom versus authoritarian dimension as on the traditional one of left versus right. Liberal and libertarian values do not make an instinctive appeal to mass electorates, any more than they do to dictatorships. They are therefore always under threat. Upholders of these values need to make use of whatever allies they can find: the identity of those allies will vary from topic to topic. Instead of heresy hunting among their own ranks, individualist liberals need to strengthen the old defences which have been built up against the group and to devise new ones. This is surely better than the slow wait for authoritarian policies to collapse under their own inadequacies.

References

Brittan, S., (1995, 1996). *Capitalism with a Human Face*. Cheltenham: Edward Elgar 1995; London: Fontana Paperback, 1996. (*See especially chapter 11 and the chart on page 253*.)

Brittan, S., and Webb, S., (1990). *Beyond The Welfare State*, Edinburgh: David Hume Institute.

Desai, M., (1997). *A Basic Income Proposal*, London School of Economics: June.

Meade, J. E., (1993). *Liberty, Equality and Efficiency*. 2nd edn, London: Macmillan.

Mill, J. S., (1859). *On Liberty*.

Turner, A., (1997). *Stakeholders, Shareholders and the Enterprise Economy*. Napier Enterprise Lecture.

Chapter Four
Justice And Reward –
Some Contractarian Thoughts*

Revival of an Old Idea

The period since 1970 has seen a revival of normative political theory: an attempt to work out consistently how individuals ought to behave towards each other in the public sphere where the compulsive agency of the state is involved.

One presupposition of this revival is that the principles of right conduct – whether between individuals or in the political sphere – are not always apparent and repay theoretical investigation. This is in contrast to the common belief that the principles are obvious – embodied in the great religious teachings or their secular equivalent – and that the only worthwhile problem is how to persuade or force human beings to conform to them more closely.

The revival has come at a price. Whereas an important minority of the educated public at one time had a smattering of the teachings of Aristotle, Locke or John Stuart Mill, the present day successors to these writers are of interest mainly to academics – and a small minority among them, mostly American or American-educated. Modern writers like John Rawls, and the early Robert Nozick have an obvious passion for public affairs. But much of the discussion has centred on the minutiae of their arguments and has been the preoccupation of a handful of postgraduates. The matters raised, are, however, too important to be left to so-called professional philosophers.

The revived interest in political ethics is closely related to a doctrine which is known by the ugly name of contractarianism. This is not one theory, but a family of theories. They are all however modern versions of the idea of the social contract which can be found in seventeenth- and eighteenth-century writers, among them John Locke and Jean-Jacques Rousseau.

A difference is that these early writers discussed a state of nature in which primitive people agreed to give up some of their freedom of action to a

*Based on Occasional Paper 6, Political Economy Research Centre, Sheffield, 1997. Incorporating material from chapter 2 of *The State Politics and Health* (ed. P Day et al) 1995.

government, or a set of rules, for the better protection of the rights which they retained. Modern writers who have retrieved the theory have dispensed with any historical or mythical gathering of this kind. Instead they start from the fact that people today have both different moral goals and different interests and desires. What then might induce people to limit the pursuit of their own goals so that they can live together without constant conflict?

Mutual Advantage

Beyond this point contractarian theories divide. The first parting of the ways is between the view of justice as mutual advantage and justice as impartiality.

Justice as mutual advantage will always be associated with the seventeenth-century British philosopher, Thomas Hobbes. Men and women in a state of nature would lead lives that would be "nasty, solitary, brutish and short". Almost any kind of government would be an improvement; and we all benefit from observing its instructions and rules, however great their shortcomings. For obedience would be better, according to Hobbes, than restarting a "warre of all against all."

Present day writers in this tradition, who often have an economics background, speak of rules that reflect the actual bargaining power of different individuals, interests and groups. James Buchanan is, if I understand him correctly, the most distinguished modern exponent.

A decisive objection to justice as mutual advantage is that it is not justice. The issue is one of substance and not just one of how we are to use words like "justice". A settlement in Bosnia based on the virtual surrender of the Bosnian Moslems may have been the best obtainable after the war in former Yugoslavia; and an international mediator could have urged it to prevent further suffering. But he would not, I hope, have had the nerve to present it as a just settlement. Mutual advantage might also have been used to support the treaties under which the American settlers deprived the original inhabitants of most of their lands.

Even if we put all these cases aside, there is a more fundamental objection. Justice as mutual advantage does not give you a reason for complying with the rules on an occasion when you believe you could get away with breaking them and thereby advance your interests more effectively. This – to my mind decisive – objection is provided by Brian Barry in the first two volumes of a projected Treatise on Social Justice.

Barry emphasises that his objection does not depend on people having exclusively selfish or material motivations. Suppose that rival religious groups, each believing it has the true faith, have fought themselves to a standstill as Catholics and Protestants did in Europe in the sixteenth and seventeenth centuries. Then, if that is all there is, each party will try to break the truce provisions when it can get away with doing so; or try to change the terms of the settlement if its own power seems to be growing – e.g. by trying to establish a Hindu state in modern India.

Sometimes a truce based on mutual advantage is all we can hope for. And where there is a rough equality between parties, the results of a self-interested contract between them may be quite similar to what is normally regarded as just. Finally and most important, even where the norms of political and personal behaviour do reflect higher moral standards, it will help to reinforce these standards if they overlap with considerations of mutual advantage. Nevertheless such considerations are only a reinforcement. Most people, some of the time, will want to justify their actions in terms that people with different interests and ideals could conceivably accept. It is this broad and empirical generalisation which makes it worthwhile to investigate alternative contractarian ideas based on the idea of impartiaiity and not mere balance of power.

Rival Original Positions?

The main rival to justice as mutual advantage is justice as impartiality. This last word reminds one of courts and the requirement that all parties should be heard on a fair and comparable basis and that no special advantage should attach to wealth, social position, ethnic group or the judge's own prejudices.

Obviously this ideal is easier to state than to achieve. But it does give us a few starting ideas. Most political philosophers who write of justice as impartiality are, however, not limiting themselves to court room procedures or narrow legal matters but have in mind the general principles – in some countries partially laid down in a constitution – by which a society is to be regulated.

For this purpose some general starting point is required. The most famous of these is the "veil of ignorance" outlined by the Harvard philosopher John Rawls. The idea is to work out the principles on which free and rational persons concerned to further their own interests would desire their community to be run if they did not know their own social or economic place, the market value of their own talents and many other key features of their real situation. If people exclude such knowledge there is some chance of formulating principles on a disinterested basis. For somebody who makes a genuine effort to work out his principles under the veil of ignorance does not know if he will be in a majority or minority group, how well off he will be or what religious principles he will profess.

Another name for the veil of ignorance is "the original position" – as it is from here that the fundamental principles of society are supposed to be derived. Those who have actually read Rawls will know that he envisages a two-way movement between our own instinctive beliefs and the definition of the original position until the two are in rough harmony with each other – a procedure which he calls reflexive equilibrium. What he is telling us to do is to embark on a thought experiment in the interests of impartiality.

The Rawls version is not the only form of contractarianism, or even the only form that stresses impartiality. It is one of a family of contractarian theories.

Many of the criticisms of the veil of ignorance are bogus objections by people who cannot understand the idea of a thought experiment. But there are real problems, One difficulty is that if we pursue impartiality far enough, we have to deprive people under the veil of ignorance of more and more information:

which country they inhabit, in which century are they living, their tastes and beliefs and, above all, their attitudes to risk and uncertainty. In the last analysis they are, as Barry says, clones or computers being fed identical programmes and producing identical results.

One alternative to the veil of ignorance might be called reasonable agreement. Its main exponent, T M Scanlon, believes that the fundamental question is "whether a principle could be reasonably rejected (for application in our imperfect world) by parties who, in addition to their own personal aims were moved by a desire to find principles that others similarly motivated could also accept." (I leave historians of thought to bring out the relationship to Immanuel Kant.)

This alternative original position has the advantage of allowing the parties to be aware of their identities and interests. Impartiality is introduced not by ignorance but by assuming them to have a desire for reasonable agreement with their fellows. The word "reasonable" does not mean rational in a logician's sense. It is given meaning by observing what counts as moral argument in real world situations where people are trying to reach a consensus and where the weighing of reasons tends to displace the counting of noses.

We can go a surprisingly long way with this procedure. But in the end the method puts too great a strain on the word "reasonable" and on people being able to agree on a common conception of what it means in different contexts.

The veil of ignorance is still to my mind the better starting point. We do not have to abstract from all our characteristics and dispositions to establish that veil. What we need to ignore depends on the question at issue. If it is the distribution of income and wealth, we need to try as far as possible to forget our own personal financial position. We do not need to be ignorant of whether we are living in the fifteenth or twenty-third centuries. If we are trying to work out an impartial law regarding religious worship we need to ask what we might advocate if we did not know our own religion or even whether we had one. We do not have to forget our age or state of health .

The Difference Principle and its Rivals

The two principles of justice which Rawls derives from the veil of ignorance are, briefly, as follows:

1. Equal rights to the most extensive scheme of equal basic liberties compatible with a similar scheme of liberties for all;

2. Social and economic inequalities must:-
   (a) work to the benefit of the least advantaged and
   (b) be attached to offices open to all.

The bulk of the discussion has been on Principle 2(a), which Rawls calls the Difference Principle, but which many economists and game theorists prefer to call the maximin: maximising the position of those with the minimum. The balance of learned discussion points to the conclusion that these particular principles, and in particular the Difference Principle, do not necessarily follow from the veil of ignorance. I observed myself in a work published at a very early stage of the debate that "the different hypothetical distributions for which people would vote, would reveal differences in their attitude to risk and uncertainty. Somebody with a taste for gambling would be interested in seeing that there were some really big incomes just in case he came out on top".

Barry attempts to improve on Rawls by deriving the Difference Principle without the aid of the veil of ignorance. One of his alternative methods is to start from the principle of equality of opportunity, which has widespread intuitive appeal. He then goes on to argue that it is not only the advantages of inherited wealth or education that load the dice against some people and in favour of others. Qualities such as intellectual ability or manual dexterity or artistic gifts have a large inborn element and may owe little to merit, effort or application. People are also affected by changes in the market for different kinds of ability which have little to do with their own efforts. The ideal of a level playing field in which people compete for unequal prizes is thus a chimaera.

Barry is of course right on these matters, although he may not like to be reminded that that arch anti-redistributionist F A Hayek made the point with great eloquence many years before:

> The inborn as well as the acquired gifts of a person clearly have a value for his fellows which do not depend on any credit due to him for possession. There is little a man can do to alter the fact that his special talents are very common or exceedingly rare. A good mind or a fine voice, a beautiful face or a skilful hand, a ready wit or an attractive personality, are in large measure as independent of a person's efforts, as the opportunities or experiences he has had.

Barry concludes that a natural or fair state of affairs is equal distribution. He then arrives at Rawlsian principles by asking what could upset the presumption in favour of equality. If every person or household received exactly the same – or even the same adjusted for the degree of pleasantness or unpleasantness (disutility) of his or her work – there would be no incentive for people to move to posts where their talents were most in demand and total wealth would therefore suffer. Even the poorest would thus gain on some departure from pure equality. But these departures should be no greater than the minimum that can be justified on incentive grounds. Neither Rawls nor Barry is at all convincing on what should determine the rewards of those who are neither at the bottom nor at the top. They both rely on the so called lexical principle: that if the poorest derive benefit from a more just organisation of society so will the decile above it, and so on into further deciles.

We are then back to the left-of-centre principle of most working social scientists and economists. Put ironically, it is that equality is the ideal; but to make the world work we require differentials of a size which benefit the academic classes and salaried professionals, but not the dreadfully high rewards gained from business or inheritance.

I resist the temptation to go into the many questions begged by the lexical principle and instead take issue with the basic presumption in favour of equality. Barry himself focuses on the key issue in a few crucial pages of his second volume, which are easily missed (pp 238–241). Assume that there are two Robinson Crusoes, A and B, on separate islands, who know of each other's existence. (Barry talks of Crusoe and Man Friday who have become separated; but the nomenclature does not affect the argument.) A turns out to be prosperous and B turns out to be living in penury, because for instance A's island is much more fertile. Neither is the cause of the other's good or bad fortune. Barry would say that the situation is unjust and that the richer A should make transfers to the poorer B to reach as near to equality as is consistent with improving B's welfare. That is the redistribution should only stop where the disincentive effect on A is so great that B ceases to gain.

There are many things that could be said about the disparity in welfare of the two Crusoes. One might say it is undesirable: or that A should transfer something to B if he has any fellow feeling. But "unjust" is hardly the word to describe the initial state of affairs, brought about neither by A nor by B nor by a third person, but by the fertility of their respective islands. If A refused to help B he might be called hard-hearted, or lacking in compassion or even callous and inhuman, but not unjust. Terminology apart, it is hardly the duty of A either to equalise conditions or (allowing for the Difference Principle) to make B as nearly well off as himself as possible. To my way of thinking, A's duty is only to raise B to something approaching the conventional minimum that both would have recognised before they were shipwrecked plus some additional amount depending on A's generosity and which cannot be determined by any *a priori* principle.

Is this the point at which Barry and I have different bedrock "ought" principles and on which we simply have to part company? A little more can be said before this point is reached. Those who believe, as Rawls and Barry both do, that the distribution of resources is ultimately a collective decision will understandably have a presumption in favour of equality, from which departures have to be justified. Those who, in the tradition of Locke, emphasise the importance of people's own efforts in creating resources which did not exist before and which are not at the expense of anyone else, have an equally understandable presumption in favour of market rewards and even inherited holdings. The model of the Locke school is the frontier pioneer who has carved his holding out of the wilderness.

Modern society is inextricably compounded of both elements. Many people do add to total wealth by their ingenuity and efforts. But they do so against a background of laws, property rights and police protection, as well as general customs, which could be different from what they are and do indeed vary from place to place. The two pictures are useful correctives to each other. But neither – nor any mixture of them – is much help on distributional issues.

Does that mean that political practitioners can relax and just accept prevailing normative principles (assuming that some can be discerned from data such as election results and opinion polls) or, more simply, follow their own hunches?

Not quite. For in contrast to Barry I find that the veil of ignorance is a more convincing starting point than either the two principles of justice which Rawls derives from that veil or Barry's own modified egalitarianism.

But however specific the veil of ignorance is made, it is unlikely to provide one indisputable set of principles for action, whether Rawls's principles of justice or any other. My own first desire under the veil of ignorance would be to make sure that everyone had a minimum income, defined not in absolute terms but in relation to the wealth of my society. This would be a safeguard in case I drew one of the unfortunate cards and found myself at the bottom of the pack. In addition, I would want to protect a large area of personal freedom where I could make my own decisions, and to ensure political, social, cultural and economic opportunities which could not be literally equal all round, but should be free of barriers of privilege and irrelevant entry qualifications. I would be disturbed by evidence that the bottom 30 per cent have gained rather little from the general rise in national income in the 1980s and 1990s, but not at all worried that indices of inequality were growing, partly because rewards at the top were rising relative to those in the middle.

Most opinion surveys are not, of course, made under the veil of ignorance or anything approaching it. When people are asked out of the blue questions of the "Who should get what?" variety, the answers are predominantly based on occupation. There is a predictable ranking, with nurses at the top and politicians, property developers and journalists at the bottom.

Some experiments have however been made with students in which they were asked to choose, among different alternatives, principles of justice which were to determine their income class. The latter was represented by an actual sum of $40 per student from which a varying deduction was made according to the counter he or she had drawn by a random process. Thus the students were constrained to choose among general income distributions and had no opportunity to express preferences for particular occupations.

For what these were worth, the experiments showed overwhelming support, not for the Rawls Difference Principle, but for maximising average income subject to a floor constraint: that is provided there was a minimum below which no one can fall. The principle is not of course a single solution, but a family of solutions governed by the choice of floor. This illustrates again the point that contractarian reasoning can reduce the differences of opinion on emotive subjects but not eliminate them altogether.

First and Second Levels

An important problem relates to the area of behaviour about which we are talking. Moral philosophers have put forward contractarian ideas in search of an interpretation of justice. But many people who have picked up some of the notions, such as Rawls's idea of maximising the well-being of the least well-off, apply them directly to public policy, without bothering whether they embody justice or some other virtue. This has been typical of economists' reactions and I plead guilty myself in applying my own principles.

Recent philosophical books on justice cover more than the principles enforced by the courts and other unwritten rules of human interaction. On the other hand, they do not intend it to cover every moral or political issue.

Barry has for instance in mind the moral and legal rules of a society, which would be "acceptable to free and equal people." but which should not determine in detail what should be done on every occasion. Some parts of the common core will be embedded in written constitutions. But this is not essential.

Of course, the demarcation between these general principles and legitimate arguments about detailed policy is itself controversial. Barry calls political and everyday decisions "first level" and the broad guidelines for public policy and personal morality "second level". There is a reason for this stress. For he is anxious to rebut accusations that justice as impartiality imposes unreasonable demands on people by requiring them to place the interests of all other persons on an equal footing, and thereby disregarding the natural tendency to pay more attention to family, loved ones and friends than to fellow citizens of one's own country or the world.

Barry would say that rescuing one's wife or child from a fire or flood, in preference to complete strangers, is acceptable as a first level principle of behaviour. But at the second or critical level, which would govern for instance public policy on flood and fire regulations, everyone's interests should count as the same unless a strong reason can be found for favouring some people over others.

The distinction between levels is familiar in utilitarian ethics or in systems such as Richard Hare's "universal prescriptivism". John Stuart Mill regarded the precepts of common sense morality, such as "Don't tell lies", as being derived from the principle of utility, that is the duty to maximise the amount of satisfaction in the world. His view was that acting directly to promote the welfare of the human race was too difficult both for the legislator and the private citizen. Both of these need the intermediate common sense generalisations. Hare argues that the best way in practice to maximise the welfare of all children is for every parent to have first and foremost the responsibility for caring for his or her own children rather than attempting the impossible tasks of caring for all the children in the world.

In such ethical systems the common sense first level precepts are clearly derived from the higher second level ones; in any conflict the latter would prevail. This position puts an enormous emphasis on being able to separate the two levels in practice. Disagreements about the level at which an issue belongs will be just as strong as disagreements about what to do at that level. For instance both egalitarians and upholders of inherited wealth and market earnings will be tempted to build into the constitution second level principles – in the one case about socially just distribution and on the other about property rights. Experience with actual constitutions and charters of human rights suggests, however, that it is hopeless to try to build into them either doctrines about just distribution or the principles of economic policy. Indeed there is no alternative to deriving them from the political process.

The most one can hope for at the constitutional or second level stage is to impose some obstacles, so that a government representing a temporary majority or plurality cannot make revolutionary changes without having to overcome some extra hurdles, such as a weighted majority, judicial review, a referendum or a second election. These constraints should apply equally to a right wing government wanting to wind down the welfare state as to a left wing one attempting to wipe out all concentrations of wealth or high earnings.

Puzzles and Worries

Finally, I come to some puzzles and worries about the contractarian enterprise.

How does contractarianism relate to David Hume's Law – that no statement about what ought to happen follows from any statement of fact or chain of logic? (You cannot derive an ought from an is.)

Contractarianism need not be a breach of Hume's Law if it is approached in a sufficiently modest spirit. Many human beings have sufficient overlap with each other in their beliefs about what they ought to do to provide a common basis for discussion. From this common ground we can proceed to argue about other issues on which people at first believe themselves to be hopelessly apart. The undertaking has a chance of progress, but only if we realise that there is no knock-down argument that can convince dissenters. The "fanatic", who turns up in almost every book of moral philosophy, will stay unconvinced.

I have, however, a genuine grouse about the expression "the good" which turns up on page after page, not only in contractarian writing but in the new political philosophy generally. It means something like: whatever goals individuals choose to pursue.

In different contexts, it seems to cover:-

(a) wants, desires and choices in the simple sense recognised by psychology and economics;
(b) personal ideals of the good life which some people will try to uphold without necessarily expecting others to follow them. The usual trivial example is to take a run every morning before breakfast; and
(c) people's moral beliefs which they would like to see regulate both public and private conduct.

There is an element of Oxford and Ivy League high-mindedness in putting these concepts together. Where political economists would talk of someone pursuing his of her self interest or expressing his or her preferences – or of maximising their utility – some political philosophers will, whenever possible, talk about following his or her idea of the good – as if simply satisfying a desire was vulgar and every action in life had to be justified by its place in the pursuit of some lofty goal.

These are deep waters in which I cannot tread much further here. But I have to explain that I find "the good" in its current philosophical use so off-putting that I try to substitute some other expression according to context, even if I am only trying to explain other people's ideas and not my own.

Conclusion

In developing contractarian ideas further, we need to move away from the preoccupation with universalism which is the hallmark of so many philosophers. In his later work Rawls goes some way to conceding that his principles are not eternal verities but embody the values of western liberal democracies. But he still opposes actual experiments and he insists that the issue is philosophical – by which he means one for armchair ratiocination by the analyst. Here he may well be wrong. However specific the veil of ignorance is made, it is unlikely to provide one indisputable set of principles for action, whether Rawls's principles of justice or any other.

Thus I return to my more general conclusion about contractarian reasoning. This is that it can help narrow – but not remove – differences on emotive subjects such as the distribution of income, wealth and power. To the extent that we can make the imaginative leap, it is a way of removing obvious bias, although not all differences of opinion. That is surely worth doing.

References

Barry, B., (1989, 1995). *Treatise on Social Justice.* Volume 1: *Theories of Justice.* London: Harvester Wheatsheaf; Volume II: *Justice as Impartiality*, Oxford: Clarendon Press

Brittan, S., (1973). *Capitalism and the Permissive Society.* London: Macmillan

Buchanan, J., (1975). *The Limits of Liberty.* Chicago: University of Chicago Press.

Frohlich, N, Oppenheimer, J. and Eavey C, (1987). Laboratory results on Rawls' distributive justice. *British Journal of Political Science*, volume 17, part 1 (January), 1–21.

Hare, R. M., (1981). *Moral Thinking.* Oxford: Clarendon Press.

Hayek, F. A., (1960). *The Constitution of Liberty.* London: Routledge.

Rawls, J., (1972). *A Theory of Justice.* Oxford: University Press,

Rawls, J., (1992). *Political Liberalism.* New York: Columbia University Press.

Scanlon, T. M., (1982). Contractualism and utilitarianism. In A Sen and B Williams (eds), *Utilitarianism and Beyond.* Cambridge: University Press.

Chapter Five
Tony Blair's Real Guru*

There was one writer who had an indisputable influence on Tony Blair when the latter was formulating his own outlook in his student years at Oxford in the early 1970s. This was the Scottish religious philosopher John Macmurray.

To some extent it was an accident that Macmurray, rather than the more usual influences such as R H Tawney, played this role. And Blair has always emphasised that it was the broad outlines rather than the details of Macmurray's arguments that he absorbed at the time. Still, it was from him that Blair believes he learned of the supposed primacy of the community over the individual.

Blair came to Macmurray in the early 1970s through Peter Thomson, an Australian Anglican vicar. Thomson was then in Oxford as a mature student (he returned to England before the 1997 election, in the first instance as vicar at St Luke's Holloway, not far from where Blair lived).

Macmurray was born in 1891 and, like many of his generation, was deeply affected by service in the trenches in the First World War. In his time, he was a highly respectable philosopher. In the 1930s he was Grote Professor of Mind and Logic in London – a chair subsequently held by the militantly anti-religious logical analyst "Freddie" Ayer. The two could not have been more different. Macmurray held the unfashionable view that philosophy should be dedicated to making sense of the universe and human life within it. The famous "linguistic turn" in English language philosophy left him high and dry. I could not find his name in any of the philosophical books I looked into, not even those dealing with personal identity, which was his special subject. American Communitarians are supposed to have rediscovered him; and the recent re-printing of several of his books must reflect something more than Blairite piety.

Macmurray's reputation suffered because, unlike most theist philosophers, he wrote in a simple and straightforward style, which increased the distrust in which he was held by other philosophers. He felt the need to establish the seriousness of his views; and the Gifford Lectures, which he gave in the early 1950s umder the general title "The Form of the Personal", were meant to be his testament.

Even today, it would be rash to underrate him. Time after time when I was tiring of his references to "Reality" or "the Other" (always in capital letters) I

* First published in *The New Statesman*, 7 February 1997.

would be stopped short by some shrewd thrust that would be hard for his opponents to parry. For instance he taxes utilitarians with advocating the maximisation of pleasure and the minimisation of pain, treating pleasure and pain as if they were the positive and negative sections of a single continuum, without realising that they are two conflicting objectives between which a choice has often to be made.

Macmurray was, above all, a natural theologian – that is, someone who tries to support religious beliefs by reason alone, without the aid of revelation, miracles or mystical experience. His approach was pretty heretical. He was cool about the standard theological proofs of the existence of God. He believed that true religion remains to be discovered, with Christianity the best approximation to date. But he was agnostic about life after death and about the Christian miracles. Indeed, he was not associated with any church until late in life, when he joined the Society of Friends.

He was always much preoccupied with the perennial argument about whether the individual is "prior" to society or society prior to the individual. To my mind this is a futile dispute. Human beings are social animals who belong to groups. Equally, groups are composed of individuals. You can look at it either way.

Macmurray, however, took the issue very seriously and tried to find a third way. For him, reality was neither the individual nor society, but personal relations. "Personal life does not exist for society. To think it does is to try to stand the world on its head . . . A citizen is something considerably lower than a person, because citizenship is only a limited aspect of a person." Sometimes he took as his model the family, and at other times pure personal friendship. For Macmurray, "religion is what a man makes of his personal relationships". God was the supreme manifestation of such relationships. It is senseless to quarrel about labels; and if a writer wants to use the word God to describe close and unconditional bonds between friends, so be it. But we are not talking about the God of Abraham, Isaac or Jacob, nor probably even the God that is worshipped in the Christian churches.

Macmurray's ideas reflected the time in which he formulated them. Personal relations were, for instance, a slogan of the Bloomsbury Group, whose members believed they had derived them from the philosopher G E Moore. The idea of personal relations being superior to either the isolated individual or the relationships characteristic of the state, politics or business, is an engaging one. But on closer examination Macmurray's version is somewhat abstract.

How does Macmurray's outlook fit in with the modern Communitarian movement? First, we have to determine what the latter is. Today's Communitarians are a vaguely defined group which has won the attention of leading politicians on both sides of the Atlantic. Albert Gore, Vice President of the USA, has warmly embraced the American Communitarian, Amitai Etzioni, while Tony Blair has mentioned approvingly the British writer, John Gray.

Communitarians are more clearly defined by what they are against than what they favour. Their highest common factor is the belief that many of the ills of our time are due to individualistic liberalism, a suspicion of Invisible Hand mechanisms and an emphasis on duty. They condemn both the minimal state liberalism formerly associated with Harvard's Robert Nozick, and the more redistributionist version associated with the rival Harvard philosopher John Rawls. Typically, Communitarians wax lyrical about neighbourhood, churches, or school authorities, and have thereby also gained the sympathy of some American "neo-conservatives" who want to distinguish their creed from classical liberalism.

All the same, anyone who, on the basis of this abbreviated sketch, expects from Macmurray the now fashionable noises in favour of "the community" and against the individual will be in for a shock. "If we say that goodness consists of serving the community, then everybody must serve. If I want to serve other people, I can't do it unless they are willing to be served. If everybody is to serve, then there is nobody to accept the service. We can't be unselfish if nobody is prepared to be selfish. If a friend and I are out walking and I have one cigarette left and he has none, then I can't act unselfishly and give it to him unless he is prepared to be selfish enough to take it from me."

Then again: "serving society or humanity always means in practice serving institutions – serving the state or your business or your trade union." Even more: "We have got to stop the false idea that it is a good idea to serve society and its institutions. The goodness of a man's life is its own quality, its integrity, not in any service it may do to other people or to the state or the church or the future."[1] I was tempted to begin this piece with some of these quotations and pretend at first that they came from Margaret Thatcher or Friedrich Hayek. But I decided to discard such debating tricks.

Macmurray was indeed opposed to what he thought of as individualism – "egocentricity become a philosophy" – an opposition on which Blair relies too much. But I am very doubtful if he was a Communitarian in the way that word is used today. Blair's interpretation of Macmurray can be found in the new Clause Four, which starts by asserting that "by the strength of our common endeavour we achieve more than we achieve alone". But this is a matter of degree. The most tightly disciplined organisation depends on some initiative on the part of its members; and even a hermit is dependent for his loin cloth on the activities of countless other human beings. The banality of the new Clause is not worthy of Macmurray or any other serious philosopher.

The danger of Communitarianism is that of attributing a superior value to collective entities over and above the individuals who compose them. This disastrous error was made respectable by the teachings of Hegel and reached its apotheosis in the state worship of the Nazi and Communist regimes, which no one denounced more vigorously than Macmurray himself, despite his sympathies with the teachings of the young Marx.

We are thus dealing with more than linguistic preferences. Behind the Communitarian talk, there are too many signs that New Labour does not attach sufficient importance to personal liberty or even to the compassion or humanity in which the real Macmurray believed. These worries about moral authoritarianism were shared by quite a few people who were working hard in Opposition with the Labour Shadow Cabinet to try to make a success of Labour's policies, and some urged me to speak out in a way they could hardly do themselves.

There was a time when liberals faced a dilemma because economic liberty was espoused mostly on the political right and personal liberty on the political left. (In the 1960s Roy Jenkins' libertarian reforms in the Home Office did more to increase individual freedom than the miserable £50 travel allowance did to destroy it.) But many of New Labour's attitudes make one wonder whether the second part of the dilemma still applies.

When Blair was a boarder at Fettes school he revolted against the harshness, lack of privacy and intrusive restrictions of his time; and rightly so. He tried to abscond at least once and, even after leaving university, he could not pass the place without it giving him the creeps. The mature Blair could have jettisoned outmoded ideological luggage, such as the old Clause Four, yet maintained his individualist rebellion against conformity and blind obedience. But this is not quite what he has done.

It is difficult to imagine Macmurray approving of a Labour leader playing court to Lee Kuan Yew of Singapore, who justifies a brutal and authoritarian regime by saying, "To us in Asia, an individual is an ant." It is also difficult to imagine him sympathising with patrols to ensure that children do specified amounts of homework laid down in a party manifesto. (One of Macmurray's addresses was to the progressive Froebel school of educationists). Nor can one imagine him wanting to sweep beggars off the street.

And I care not to contemplate how he would have reacted to Labour's long hesitation in opposing the original version of the last Conservative Government's Police Bill, its silence on the barbaric habit of putting prisoners into chains, or its failure to denounce instantly and directly (as distinct from making political capital out of the inept handling of) the attempt of the last Conservative Education Secretary, Gillian Shephard, to bring back beating into state schools.

Despite all my reservations about Macmurray's type of metaphysics, Tony Blair should read him again rather than simply treat his presence on his bookshelves as an inspiration. Some warning signals would surely emerge.

Books by John Macmurray:

Freedom in the Modern World, Faber, 1932.
All the following are Faber reprints, 1995:
Reason and Emotion
The Form of the Personal
  1 *The Self as Agent*
  2 *Persons in Relation.*

PART II

THE CHANGING WORLD ECONOMY

Chapter Six
Globalisation: Myth And Reality*

Demonisation

A former political adviser to President Clinton, one James Carville, remarked: "I used to think, if there was reincarnation, that I wanted to come back as the president or the Pope or a baseball hitter. But I now want to come back as the bond market. You can intimidate everyone."

This is a typical piece of demonisation. Another example was provided in 1993 when the French franc suffered a speculative attack and the old narrow band Exchange Rate Mechanism collapsed. The Finance Minister at the time, Michel Sapin, blamed the weakness of the franc on *agiteurs* (political speculators) whose forebears had been beheaded during the French Revolution.

Both these embittered reactions make the fatal mistake of treating the financial markets – which represent the reactions of millions of people to millions of disparate events – as if they were the work of a single player holding the world in the palm of his hand. It is the classic mistake of blaming the messenger when we do not like the news he or she brings.

Those Overnight Markets

Some aspects of modern changes are much exaggerated. An example is the way speakers try to make their audiences' flesh creep with estimates of the turnover of the foreign exchange market, estimated at well over $1,000bn per day.

Such huge numbers are often used as a conversation stopper. You can prove what you like with them. If you are a Euro-sceptic you can ask how European currencies can be permanently brought together in the face of flows of such magnitude. If you are a fan of Monetary Union you can ask what sense it makes for national governments to try to maintain independent currencies and independent monetary policies against flows of this kind.

The fact is that the vast bulk of this trillion dollars consists of mutually offsetting very short term transactions, which are reversed within a day or even within a few minutes. Instability comes about when it requires large

* A revised and extended version of an essay first published in *Parliamentary Brief*, July 1996.

movements in the price of the different currencies to clear the markets at the end of the day or week. But that was equally true when Stafford Cripps was forced to devalue the pound in 1949.

What's New?

Demonisation aside, a change has indeed come over the world economy which is often called globalisation, although it has many other properties.

Globalisation proper has two main features: – the reduction or elimination of barriers to trade between countries and areas; and the liberalisation of capital markets so that you can move investible funds to whichever part of the world where returns seem highest.

Some academic economists ask: what is new about these developments? They argue that we have simply gone back to the world which prevailed before World War One when there were no exchange or capital controls and net overseas investment was in some countries a higher proportion of national income than it is today.

But even if we were merely seeing a return to the conditions of nearly a century ago, this would still be noteworthy. For it would be right outside the experience of every active market participant or official who started work before the 1990s. However suspicious we may be of spurious revolutions, proclaimed in economic potboilers, we still have a feeling in our bones that some things are different to what they were even before 1914.

The cliche answer to what is new is to say Information Technology (IT). Obviously the ability, not merely to move funds to the remotest parts of the world, but to obtain on a screen information or misinformation on what is going on there is an important change. But it is surely less important than the invention of the transatlantic cable which transmitted to the New York Stock Exchange news of the financial crash in Vienna in 1873. The leap from laborious horse-drawn transport and sailing ships to the railways and transatlantic cable was a bigger jump than that from the cable to modern information technology.

A more plausible candidate is the switch in the kinds of trade. The bulk of nineteenth-century exchanges still consisted of the sale of food and raw materials for manufactured goods. Today most trade consists of the specialised interchanges of manufactures and services. A related aspect is the rise of multinationals which can easily switch operations from one part of the globe to another. A bigger difference is that at the end of the nineteenth century there were still vast open spaces in North America and elsewhere where workers from the Old World could go if their domestic prospects were unsatisfactory. There is now no place where US unskilled workers, whose wages are under pressure, can find a similar escape.

There is also a greater geographical difference compared with the late nineteenth century. At that time only the coastal fringes of Asia and Africa were drawn into the global trade and payments system, which was centred on Europe. Now, following the collapse of Soviet-style communism and Third

World belief in central planning, billions more people are being drawn into a single world economy – most of all, of course India and China but also Latin America, the Asian Tigers, many parts of Africa and of course the former members of the Soviet bloc in Europe.

Lastly, there is a change in the nature of modern capitalism worth mentioning, namely the resurgence of the private investor. David Hale of Zurich Kemper Investments estimates that 37 per cent of all US households hold investments in at least one mutual fund. The shift in the UK from earnings-related pensions to pension related to the value of invested contributions is likely to generate, if not direct equity ownership, at least a much greater interest in the performance of equities on which future pensions will depend.

The Mythical Powerlessness of Governments

The limits all these changes impose on national policy are probably less than it is fashionable to suppose.

It is often asserted that globalisation imposes financial orthodoxy, for instance that the financial markets will punish any government that runs a sizeable deficit. In fact the reason why some European Governments went to heroic lengths to reduce Budget deficits in the 1990s was to qualify for European Monetary Union under the Maastricht rules. Globalisation had little to do with it.

What happens in a unified world capital market if, for whatever reason, a government, not affected by Maastricht considerations, runs a substantial deficit? Assume too, for the sake of argument, that the government still wants to avoid inflation or that there is an independent central bank that is intent on doing so, and that interest rates are therefore raised. Funds will be attracted from overseas and the currency may actually rise, as occurred in the US in the early Reagan period. This can actually exert a stabilising experience on the internal economy. For any stimulus given by the deficit is offset by dearer money and lost competitiveness overseas.

In the longer run the analysis becomes much more complicated. Suppose the deficit is too large or maintained for too long. Eventually international investors will begin to worry about the future of the currency and in extreme cases about the possibility of government debt repudiation. When this happens the exchange rate will plunge, and the government may well have to tighten fiscal or monetary policy or both to prevent a downward currency spiral.

To some of us who remember earlier sterling crises the process is quite familiar. The old sterling area, whose member countries held reserves in London, first masked and then magnified the effect of domestic overheating. The masking came because small increases in the Bank Rate attracted enough funds to London to cover quite large payments deficits; but eventually confidence was lost and there was a run out of sterling.

The conclusion is straightforward. With active international capital markets, a budget deficit can be comfortably financed for a surprising while. But when nemesis arrives it is all the more sure.

Let us modify the above example and suppose that the government is prepared to have a higher rate of inflation than its trading partners. It may do so because it hopes (probably in vain) that it will thereby expand output and employment. The toleration of inflation will undoubtedly mean higher nominal interest rates and a depreciating currency. In highly metaphorical terms, the overseas holders of funds may be said may be said to be punishing governments. In fact, they are merely asking for a higher nominal return to cover the risk of depreciation.

Old Rules Still Apply

The economic case for globalisation is that it has enabled countries with high rates of savings and relatively low returns on investment to lend to others with low savings but a higher return on capital.

Cratefuls of airport bestsellers have been written denouncing globalisation, based on elementary errors of fact or logic. Speakers at business or political conferences can win cheap applause by saying that all the old rules of economics no longer apply. They rarely pause to tell us what these decried old rules actually are. As the shrewder observers of the global economy point out, the new worldwide market in fact increases the importance of these rules. (See for instance, L Bryan and D Ferrell 1996.)

Some demagogues ask – as if were a new and profound question – how western countries can hope to compete with others where wages are a tenth or a 50th as high. These specific fractions come from bar-room gossip. The fact is that countries with very different levels of technologies, wages and other variables have long managed to trade with each other to their mutual profit. The key principle of international trade – laid down nearly two centuries ago by the British economist David Ricardo – is that countries can trade with each other even if one of them has a cost advantage in every single product.

Trade does not depend on one country being absolutely better or more efficient in producing a particular product. It would pay Norway to export fish and import bananas, even if hothouse technology reached a point where bananas could be grown more efficiently north of the Arctic circle than on the Equator.

Why did it pay some countries in the nineteenth century to export wheat and import machinery? Not necessarily that they were more efficient in growing wheat than their trading partners. Even if a country is more efficient at both growing wheat and producing machinery, its citizens would enjoy a higher standard of living if they can transform wheat into machinery by selling in the international market rather than remaining self-sufficient. What is important is not the cost of one country compared with another, but the ratio of the costs of making one product to the cost of making another in the *same* country. So long as these ratios differ internationally it pays to trade.

This simple matter of logic and arithmetic makes nonsense of the claim of populist economists that the United States and Europe face a huge competitiveness threat from the emerging countries. Such pop economists assert that the low wages paid in emerging countries will undermine prosperity and destroy jobs on a massive scale unless we pull our socks up and engage in a mass of frenetic activities, ranging from so-called industrial policy to back door protectionism. Such assertions are based on the fallacy that countries are entities like Coca Cola and Pepsi Cola that compete with each other in essentially a zero sum game. Not so. The growth of the emerging economies is not a threat but an opportunity.

The pop economist cannot have it both ways. As Krugman has pointed out, if the emerging countries attract vast amounts of investment from the West, they cannot at the same time have large export surpluses. By definition, the gap between exports and imports equals the gap between savings and investment. The emerging countries may attract inward investment, in which case they will run trade deficits, not surpluses. Or they will run surpluses, but then they will export capital to, and not import it from, the West. This follows from the elementary accounting identities which everyone – including industrialists who complain of a competitiveness threat – employ in their own businesses.

What about low wages? Are not they a threat to western nations? No. Wages reflect, at a first approximation, the average level of efficiency in an economy. If wages are low in a high tech Chinese factory, it is because the average level of productivity in China is also low. There will be plenty of sectors left where higher US wages are offset by greater efficiency. Prof. Richard Freeman of Harvard has estimated (cited by Rodrik) that 80 per cent of the differential between US and Mexican workers is asssociated with overall skill differences, and differences between market exchange rates and relative purchasing power.

There is always a real exchange rate at which a high wage country can compete with a low wage one. Let us take a country such as the Czech Republic which we could visit in a few hours. It has much lower wages than its western neighbours such as Germany. This is a measure of the temporary backwardness of its economy after decades of Communist rule. But the Czechs do not sell abroad to line their Government offices with D-mark, dollar or Euro notes. They sell abroad to pay for vital imports or to service the interest on overseas borrowing. So despite Pat Buchanan and James Goldsmith, the advanced industrial countries still gain from trade with less advanced ones.

But what is true is that the gains from globalisation accrue unevenly to different sections in the advanced countries, and perhaps accrue more to capital than to labour. In any case wage gaps between advanced and emerging countries have been narrowing and will continue to do so. It could be that the trend towards wage equalisation will occur through wages in these countries rising rather than wages of less skilled workers in the west falling. But on some assumptions – such as highly competitive labour markets in China or India – this need not happen for a long time. In that case the gains will accrue to Chinese workers not previously fully employed or to the owners of capital. There is still no reason for the West as a whole to do anything but gain. But the distributional problems in the West will be much greater.

For an unwelcome development as the twentieth century draws to its close has been the widening of market-based income differentials within advanced industrial countries. How far this development is related to globalisation and how far to domestic technical change is a matter of dispute, which will not be readily resolved.

One of the most sophisticated critiques of globalisation – from the US economist Dan Rodrik – centres on this point. His main argument is that, until recently, trade liberalisation was accompanied by an expansion in the Welfare State to act as a cushion against competitive shocks. Now, however, globalisation makes it difficult to tax corporations effectively at above the going world rate. But it also makes it politically hard (although not in my view impossible) to tax labour incomes instead, because of the downward pressures it may be exerting on the real wages of less skilled workers. These problems have already been touched upon in Chapter Three, and will be taken up again in Chapter Seven on the Welfare State.

Financial Crises

It is unfortunate that most of the serious writing on globalisation comes from international trade specialists. For the biggest strains on the system have come from volatile capital flows. The three main crises, up to the time of writing, have been the Latin American one of 1982, the Mexican Tequila one of 1994–95 and the East Asian insolvencies that emerged in 1997. They have all had different origins. And the problems of Japan, which maintains a high current balance of payments surplus, have not been not those of globalisation at all. They have been the combination of an ill-performing banking system, bolstered by too much official protection, and an excessively restrictive macroeconomic policy aggravated for several years by misguided American pressure for yen appreciation.

What the genuine globalisation crises have in common has been an excessive pile-up of overseas borrowing, often to finance unsustainable property and equity booms, followed by equally excessive disinvestment as lenders have lost confidence. They have been also been aggravated by the domino effect as the fall from favour of one emerging country has tempted the financial markets to look for the next victim.

One consolation from the Asian financial crises that developed in the winter of 1997–98 is that we should now hear much less about East Asian countries having invented a non-individualistic form of capitalism superior to the self-centred hedonistic kind enjoyed in the West. We should hear less praise for the close relations – now called crony capitalism – between government and business in many of these countries and the element of central guidance behind their development. What events have shown is that, so far from having developed a superior model, some of the most highly praised East Asian economies are prone to all the excesses of the Anglo-Saxon form of capitalism and then some more. They have developed bubble economies with an over-indulgence in real estate and stock market investment, driven by lax bank lending policies as well as over-optimism by foreign investors. (At one time the aggregate market value of real estate in Greater Tokyo was estimated to be larger than that of all the property in the US.)

Asian growth is indeed likely to resume after adjustments have been made. What is over is the so-called Asian model as a system of organisation of which western countries should either be terrified of, or attempt to emulate. Above all there is no more need to be impressed by the results supposedly achieved by the short way adopted by many Asian regimes with critics of authority, the resolute suppression of "permissive" lifestyles and the draconian punishments for minor offences.

It is now clear that the phase of very rapid growth in parts of East Asia has much in common with comparable growth rates experienced by the defunct Soviet Union, which were too often taken at face value. Even the Nobel prize economist Paul Samuelson once predicted that Soviet living standards would catch up with those of America by the early 1990s. Soviet growth was genuine enough, but based on the forced injection of capital and western technology, which provide only a one shot boost. Authoritarian arrangements do not encourage innovation or adaptation.

Meanwhile, there are several ways in which debt crises such as those of East Asia, can affect the rest of the world. The trade effects, as these countries are forced to import less and export more are the most obvious, but also the easiest to play down by establishment economists. More important is the increased suspicion that falls on other debtors throughout the world.

Another danger is that contagion from Asia could affect American and other equity values, which were already too high by 1997 by many criteria. It will be almost impossible to disentangle a healthy correction from the early stages of a self-feeding downward spiral. Most worrying of all would be a more general loss of business confidence in the West. It is precisely when there are no indications of this to be seen that policy-makers need to be eagle-eyed for warning signals.

The biggest responsibility undoubtedly falls on the main industrial countries, who are in a position to offset any worldwide contraction in demand emanating from Asia or elsewhere. This is made unnecessarily difficult because of the current central bank fashion for concentrating only on foreseeable domestic inflation as measured by one particular set of fallible consumer price indices. Western policy-makers need to reassert their responsibility for maintaining world nominal demand.

I should not need to add that as the emerging countries adjust their econo-mies, some deterioration in the current account of Western countries needs to be accepted. If we could only rely on these common sense responses we could enjoy a great benefit from globalisation as, in the IMF's words, world-level fluctuations would be "dampened owing to the lack of synchronisation of disturbances across national economies and a partial absorption by external imbalances".

The maintenance of nominal demand in the West is a necessary, but not a sufficient, condition for the smoother operation of world capitalism. Attention also needs to be paid to the type of adjustment being urged on East Asian countries. Many of them operated pegged exchange rates for far too long. When funds were coming in to feed an unsustainable boom, interest rates could not be raised for fear of currency appreciation. When the boom was punctured they had to be raised excessively in a vain effort to stop an outflow.

Nevertheless a policy of benign neglect of the exchange rate rarely works. An exchange rate in free fall in an open emerging economy can do much harm. It squeezes already vulnerable living standards. More specifically, the countries affected have to export or borrow far more to service an existing volume of dollar-denominated debt. If domestic financial institutions have dollar debts that exceed the foreign exchange reserves of the country concerned, its own central bank is not able to prevent a collapse of the financial system. Thus even in a floating world there is still be need for an international lender of last resort.

There is no need to be dogmatic about whether governments or central banks should assume leadership or the precise role that institutions such as the IMF should play. But leadership can only come – as in all other spheres – from a very small group. We could start off with the existing Group of Seven summit countries, reformed to reduce the excessive European representation and the unnecessary presence of Canada. Room would thus be made for East Asian and Latin American representatives, together with someone from the former Communist world.

However little economic intervention one believes in, that little needs to be on a much bigger scale than that of the individual country or even the Euro bloc. There is an enormous confusion between views of how much government we need and its geographical extent. So long as there is a small specialised high quality staff, the political oversight can be exercised by the heads of the most important governments acting on a confederal basis without supranational authority. It is good fun inventing new institutions, with even more economic advisers. But it is simpler and quicker to use the ones we already have.

Postscript: Keynes and Globalisation

Every day, some international organisation or national think tank lectures us on the need to save more. What would happen if a country took this advice to heart? The most likely response would be firm action to reduce budget deficits, which count as negative savings.

According to both classical economists and traditional moralists, the results could be nothing but beneficial. Interest rates would fall, investment rise and the growth rate increase. As a result, citizens would before long be more than compensated for their temporary sacrifices.

It was the achievement of the British economist, John Maynard Keynes (1883–1946) to demonstrate that these moralising tales might not always be true. The traditional analysis, by focusing only on interest rates, overlooked another variable which might respond, namely output and employment. An attempted increase in savings might reduce national income and raise unemployment. This could happen because interest rates fail to fall enough, or because investment is not sufficiently sensitive to interest rates. The result might, therefore, be a recession rather than an investment boom.

This bald summary leaves open many questions. How likely is such a savings-induced slump? Can it lead to a long-lasting under-employment equilibrium; or are self-correcting forces likely to come to the rescue in the longer term? And is official intervention to try to offset swings in private savings and in investment likely to help, or to be so perverse in timing as to make matters worse rather than better?

These and many other related questions have been endlessly debated in the 60 and more years since Keynes's *General Theory* appeared and are no nearer resolution. Answers are likely to depend on particular circumstances of time and place. Nevertheless Keynes succeeded in showing that an attempted increase in savings *can* have depressive effects, and not just the virtuous ones previously claimed. Here is his main contribution to economic understanding for which he would have deserved the Nobel Prize – had it existed for his subject in his lifetime – several times over.

There has been a tendency to obscure the matter by too much talk of Keynes's wider vision, or his view of government, or his role in the Bloomsbury group of artists and writers. But without the General Theory and its over-saving doctrines, Keynes would be remembered mainly by historians for his critique of the Versailles Treaty and his name would not be a household word today.

There is, incidentally, no incompatibility between the General Theory and the main doctrine of the classical counter-revolution. The latter is embodied in the so-called natural rate of unemployment, more politely known as the NAIRU (non-accelerating inflation rate of unemployment). This doctrine maintains that if governments try to reduce unemployment below a minimum level, the result will just be accelerating inflation. That minimum depends on labour market characteristics and cannot be avoided by putting more money into the economy. The General Theory warns however that you might not get unemployment even as low as the natural rate if attempted savings are too high and demand is, therefore, inadequate.

This potted summary of two generations of theorising has been given, not for its own sake but for its relevance to the globalisation debate. Globalisation refers to a world in which, after allowing for exchange rate and default risk, there is a single international rate of interest. What effect does globalisation have on the likelihood of Keynesian over-saving? To start with, the interest rate safety valve is removed. For if real interest rates are determined globally a country cannot respond to higher attempted savings by its residents by means of lower interest rates. (For some elaboration and qualification of this thesis, see Brittan, 1996, chapter 9.) But another, and probably more important, safety valve comes to replace it. The key point is that a normal country's savings or investment is only a small part of the world's total. Suppose that a country tries to increase its savings and there are no immediate domestic investment opportunities for which they can be used. It can invest the surplus overseas instead. Under the conventions of national income book-keeping an increase in overseas investment is identical with a shift towards surplus in the current balance of payments of the same amount. If matters work out well the effect of individuals or governments trying to save more is an increase in overseas assets.

There is no reason in principle why the Japanese savings surplus should not be offset by an increase in overseas assets for a good many years, until the time comes in the twenty-first century when the changing demographic balance of the population leads to a large drop in savings. This could be accomplished without recession and provide a nest egg for the much larger number of old people then expected. The main reason why Japan has had such difficulty in maintaining a high savings equilibrium is that the yen exchange rate was for so long perversely high. This could have been reversed much earlier than it was by an easier money policy – if necessary by printing yen to buy dollars. (In a global economy, an easy money policy makes itself felt through a lower nominal exchange rate.)

One reason why Japan has found such a logical policy difficult to follow is the economic illiteracy of so many American policy-makers, who have regarded the Japanese payments surplus as a threat rather than a way of financing more world investment than would otherwise be possible. Indeed, for many years the US positively welcomed a soaring yen in the hope that it would reduce Japanese competitiveness.

The Keynesian threat of over-saving can still come back, however, to haunt us on the international scene. All countries cannot run payments surpluses. (If we had accurate figures, international oayments imbalances would sum to zero.) So it is still possible to have a Keynesian-type slump in a global economy.

The International Monetary Fund has tried to take on board these concerns by projecting the effects of lower budget deficits (equivalent to higher saving) both in the US, and in the rest of the developed world taken together. The main effect on which the IMF relies to offset the depressive effects of lower deficits is a fall in real interest rates. It reckons that the increase in Government debt ratios among developed countries has raised the average level of world real interest rates by at least 11/2 percentage points. It expects that a reduction in debt and deficits would help reverse the trend – although only the US is a large enough part of the world economy for a one-country increase in savings to have perceptible effect on the going international interest rate.

In any case, this effect takes time. Even on the IMF simulation, there is a year or two after a US stabilisation programme starts in which output is depressed on Keynesian lines both in America and in the rest of the world. If this setback occurs in the aftermath of a world recession or disappointing recovery, there could still be a danger of triggering off a cumulative depression. Given the uncertainties of the models, we should be relieved that countries are likely to try to stabilise their Budgets or raise their private savings ratios, a few at a time, rather than in one fell swoop. A worldwide spread of fiscal virtue could be disastrous.

References

Brittan, S., (1995, 1996). *Capitalism with a Human Face*. Cheltenham: Edward Elgar, 1995; London: Fontana paperback, 1996.
Bryan, L., and Ferrell, D., (1996). *Market Unbound*. New York: John Wiley.
International Monetary Fund, (1997). World Economic Outlook: Interim Assessment, December, Washington.

Krugman, P., (1997). *Pop Internationalism*. Cambridge Mass. and London: MIT Press.

Rodrik, D., (1997). *Has Globalisation Gone Too Far?* Washington, Institute for International Economics.

Lingle D., (1997). *The Rise and Decline of the Asian Century*. Sirocco Publishers, Barcelona.

Chapter Seven
The Labour Market
And The Welfare State*

Main Challenges

The financial problem of the Welfare State is most acute in Continental Europe. It has been kept at bay in Britain partly by demographic good fortune and partly by the measures taken by the Thatcher Governments to link benefits to inflation rather than to real incomes.

But the issues still matter, even from a parochial point of view. The UK's fortunes are bound up with those of other members of the European Union. Moreover, the problems which are expressed as budgetary ones on the Continent are expressed in Britain in terms of concern about the adequacy of welfare provision.

A few remarks were made at the end of Chapter Three on services in kind such as health and education. This chapter is mainly concerned with cash transfers. But it also looks at some of the emerging problems of the labour market left over from the discussion of globalisation. Many European countries have faced a crisis of government spending and public debt. The typical ratio of general government outlays to GDP rose from 35 per cent in 1970 to over 50 per cent in the early 1990s. Welfare spending of all kinds, and social security spending in particular, were the main, although of course not the only, reasons for this increase.

We have now reached the stage where we have to run fast to stay where we are. In many industrial countries the Budget deficit approached 5 per cent of GDP before the emergency spending curbs enforced by the Maastricht Treaty "convergence" requirements – deficit levels previously only seen during major wars and in the Great Depression. These were associated with leaps in debt ratios. So if the Maastricht criteria and the EMU Stability Pact had not been devised for the purposes of European Monetary Union, they would still have had to be invented to prevent an explosive debt trap. By a debt trap I mean a position where deficits increase continuously, or taxation has to rise for the

*An early version of this chapter first appeared in Henry Cavanna (ed), *Challenges to the Welfare State*, Cheltenham: Edward Elgar, 1998.

foreseeable future, not to finance increased primary spending, but simply to service the debt on past borrowing.

Unfortunately, dealing with existing deficits is only the beginning. Because of the ageing of the population, contributions or taxes will have to increase or entitlements reduced, simply to close the contribution gap in the main European social security funds. This gap has been put by the IMF at 3 to 3½ per cent of GDP for France and Germany, but only 0.1 per cent for the UK. These Continental gaps represent large sums. To plug them would require the raising of personal tax rates by 7 percentage points or other equivalent measures.

Many observers of the European scene, especially on the employers' side, make matters too easy for themselves by putting all the blame on high social security overheads which can add 50 per cent or more to their wage bills. Occasionally they advocate "fiscalisation" – that is the transfer of the cost of social security to the general tax system.

In fact, nothing is fundamentally changed if welfare benefits are paid for by direct taxes rather than social security levies. The process is simply less transparent. The tensions arise if workers do not value the "social wage" sufficiently and regard the taxes raised to pay for it as a wedge between their gross earnings and take-home pay. They will then either work less at the margin or exert pressure for higher pay, which it might require high unemployment to offset. This is all elementary economic analysis in which the word "globalisation" does not even have to be mentioned.

What lies behind very high Continental "welfare" claims on resources? Many influences have been at work: improved benefits, demographic shifts and changed social attitudes which have led to a greater take-up. Above all, benefit entitlements were decided on the basis of more optimistic economic growth assumptions than would today be regarded as realistic.

The Ageing Problem

Contrary to popular myth, less than 8 per cent of British benefit expenditure is devoted to the unemployed, whether in the form of contributory benefit or means-tested Income Support. The great bulk of spending goes to the old and the sick.

TABLE 7.1   UK BENEFIT EXPENDITURE

	1997–1998 Estimates £m.
Elderly people	42,430
Long-term sick and disabled	23,940
Short term sick	1,210
Family	18,740
Unemployed people	7,160
Widows and others	2,240
Total benefit expenditure	**95,730**

Source: Social Security Departmental Report 1997

The burden of providing for the old is due partly to the ageing of the postwar baby boom and partly to an increase in life expectancy. So far this has not been matched by a later retirement age, at least for men. On the contrary it has been aggravated by a trend to early retirement or departure from the working population by workers in late middle age or even younger. It is this pressure which leads to the alarming deficit projections on the Continent and to a skimpy state pension in the UK.

By far the most important contribution that could be made to the state pension problem would be to raise the age of retirement. This takes a few seconds to say, but would have enormous implications. It would reverse many of the effects of demography and reduce the burden of caring for the old. On the IMF estimate, raising the normal German retirement age to 67 would eliminate completely the contribution deficit. Even in Britain the indexation of the retirement age to life expectancy of a person in his or her sixties from the inception of the postwar scheme would have saved about £8 billion per annum, or 20 per cent, of the present cost of benefits for the old.[1]

The demonstration effects would extend further. Private pension schemes would be influenced towards a higher retirement age. Moreover both employers and older workers would tend to have a different attitude if the reference point for retirement was 67 rather than 60 or 65. The ideal would be to have no standard retirement age and to leave it to individual decisions.

Low Pay

At least as important a social problem as that of pensions is that of growing differentials in market-clearing rates of pay. The victims are the unlucky and the unskilled. In some countries these pressures express themselves in low pay; and in others, where pay is held up by collective agreements or labour market regulation, it is expressed in high unemployment. It is too simple to say that it is the highly skilled who will escape this problem. Krugman[2] has made some intriguing but plausible predictions that those whose services will be in the greatest demand in decades to come will not be the computer specialists of official imagination, but workers such as home health and care aides, gardeners or helpers looking after children, whom robots are not going to replace for a very long time, if ever.

The distinction between the problem of ageing and that of unemployment is in fact not clear-cut. For there is an intermediate category: the "discouraged"

TABLE 7.2   EXPECTANCY OF LIFE (YEARS) ENGLAND AND WALES

| | Males | | Females | |
	At birth	Age 65	At birth	Age 65
1841	40.2	10.9	42.2	11.5
1950–52	66.4	11.7	71.5	14.3
1993–95	74.1	14.6	79.4	18.3

Source: ONS

workers who are not officially unemployed, but have left the labour force, usually after losing their jobs, at well below the normal pension age. Such inactive middle-aged people may live on invalidity, or sickness benefits, but very often they will have an occupational pension or be supported by a wife or husband who is at work. They will mostly have paid off their mortgages and be able to live on lower take-home pay than younger citizens. The inactivity of so many people of working age is not only a social problem. It represents an unpardonable waste at a time when the dependency ratio is in any case growing. We are, as it were, throwing away the contributions of many people who, with a little encouragement, would still like paid work.

Minimum Income Guarantee

The effects of these distributional forces are pervasive. I have already discussed the idea of some form of minimum income guarantee in Chapter Three. The cost of such a guarantee, and its disincentive effects, are least when there is a large gap between the wages of typical low-paid workers and what would be regarded as a decent subsistence minimum. When pay is itself very low, the costs of such a scheme rise, and, with them, the danger that it would provide many people with a disincentive to seek paid work. This was believed to be the effect of the Speenhamland system introduced by the British magistrates in 1795 under which local justices of the peace were supposed to make payments to supplement the pay of agricultural workers.

Even though a full basic or citizen income is at present out of reach, I would still like to make a start and introduce at least a small unconditional payment to everyone to keep the principle alive. Such a modest payment could still make the difference for some people between a life full of negotiation with social security officers and one which they can call their own. There are always bound to be gaps and injustices in social security schemes which depend either on contribution records or which are means-tested in one way or another. An automatic over-the-counter payment would enable everyone to have a very basic minimum without having to satisfy complicated criteria or having to tell public officials all about his or her private circumstances.

I have been attracted to the minimum income idea for many reasons. First and foremost I would like to reduce the puritan element in capitalist culture by allowing everyone a choice to live on a modest but survivable income if he or she wants to opt out of the conventional rat race. Such an income would also help people in the beginning of their careers who wanted to take risks or work part-time while they developed their real talents. Many such people are not eligible for conventional grants or do not know how to apply for them.

Of more immediate relevance is that if there were a minimum income it would be possible to oppose minimum wage legislation, or indeed all the collective bargaining practices which divorce an individual's pay from his or her market rate of pay, and to do so with a clear conscience. It is surely better to supplement low pay with top-up benefits than to price people out of work and then pay them the dole for doing nothing. We can move in this direction incrementally, even before a full Basic Income comes within reach. The Conservative Family Benefit and Labour's Working Families Tax Credit have been steps in this direction. It is now important to extend these benefits to households without children. But probably the harshest aspect of present income-related benefits is the very severe test of capital means, which could be lightened somewhat without opening the floodgates to abuse.

Relevance of Globalisation

There is far more to be said on all the detail. But I do not think the main outlines of Welfare State problems will change very quickly. So I would like to turn to the question, how far are the problems of the Welfare State affected by globalisation? By this I mean primarily the new freedom for capital movements and trade to go wherever the return seems highest. This is caricatured by those who dislike the supposed dominance of the bond markets. But a more straightforward way of putting it is that the world is becoming a single economy.

The system which might be called the Social Market has been based on a compromise. Workers are paid the market rate of return. But very adverse impacts on low incomes are in principle offset by cash transfers. This is so whether the transfers come from a conventional social security system or from some form of basic or minimum income guarantee. Such transfers are of course between citizens. The state is only an agency and has no resources of its own. The nagging question is: will those who are net payers accept the loss in their take-home pay? Or will they be able to pass on the cost of their tax and social security payments so that there is nothing left to redistribute? In a traditional parochial economy passing-on has been limited. For the essential assumption was that workers were immobile between countries. A relatively well-paid citizen who was taxed to finance a top-up payment for poorer workers had not much choice but to accept most of the burden. He might at the margin have worked a little less, but he would have found it difficult to escape the transfer altogether.

In the early stages of the global economy one may assume that mobility of labour is still limited, in line with existing European evidence. In that case it will still be possible to offset some of the tendency towards bigger income differentials. But that will apply only as far as they affect the relativities of different sorts of worker. The grave problems will arise if there is not merely an adverse trend in the pay of low skilled or unlucky workers. Let us suppose that there is also a fall in the return to labour in general relative to the return to capital. This is certainly possible in a world of capital shortage, which has so far only been a threat but may yet develop.

Capital is by definition mobile in a global economy. One country can still have higher rates of tax on profits than another. But it must then allow a pattern of pay, prices and exchange rates which will enable companies working in that country to enjoy the going world *net post-tax* rate of return. If a government tries to stop this, not only will it fail to attract outside capital, but existing domestic companies will shift more of their investment abroad.

The more ownership of capital can be spread among the mass of citizens, the less will this fiscal inhibition matter. For the going rate of return will be available to a pension fund-holder in a small village in the Tatra mountains as well as to an international dealer in Zurich. Devices such as pension funds, especially when individually owned, or worker shares, are all helpful here. The problem is that the bottom third or half of the population tend to be outside all such schemes.

Job Insecurity

The most discussed aspect of the new capitalism is job insecurity. This has been aggravated by the macho fashion for "lean management", corporate restructuring, out-sourcing and the like. Some of the prophets of this style have since had second thoughts. Perhaps more enduring is the feeling that people will not be able to stay in one job for most of their lives, but will either occupy many different post or move to small service companies which undertake a great variety of tasks for many different final purchasers. As an *Economist* survey has shown, it is surprisingly difficult to find hard statistical evidence of shorter job tenure. But it could still happen: and even the fear that jobs are insecure can be a potent source of misery.

Let us consider risk-averse individuals who are attracted by the old idea of a lifetime career in a single organisation and do not take kindly either to working for themselves or to frequent changing of jobs. Let us suppose that in today's world it does really cut costs for companies to hive off many activities and to purchase their materials, components and even organisational skills from outside. Now none of these matters is absolute. Everything turns on the cost of having something done in-house compared to that of buying it in. Let executives or others who value long-term employment offer themselves for less than their fellows to encourage employers make use of their services. The whole idea of undercutting, whether in wages or prices, is still found shocking by many people, as is the idea of paying different amounts for apparently similar services. But if human beings have different preferences and desires, it makes sense to have pay patterns which enable them to realise them. After all it was traditional for people who were risk-averse to join the Civil Service or become teachers for a more certain but lower reward. I am simply suggesting extending this principle to business employment itself. Indeed it will happen once people have made the mental leap.

Of course there are difficulties. The old-fashioned long-term employment with a firm was not normally expressed in an implicit contract. It was simply assumed that if the employee performed adequately and the firm suffered no abnormal setbacks, the principle of first-in last-out would be followed. If a recruit is to be expected to work for lower pay something more explicit might be required.

Nightmare or Utopia?

Let me end this not altogether cheerful chapter with a vision which some will regard as a utopia and others as a nightmare. The situation, in which capital is mobile and labour is not, is hardly permanent. Movements across the Rio Grande between Mexico and the United States are surely suggestive of what will happen in Europe. It is inconceivable that growing populations in North Africa, enjoying more and more media information on European life, will simply accept a large adverse disparity in living standards without doing something about it. Migration, whether legal or illegal, is about the most peaceful move they might attempt. The prospect of fundamentalist Moslem governments is likely to make movement even greater, as there will be many millions who will prefer the rewards of this world to the austere consolations of the faith. There are also likely to be many attempts to move from a chaotic and disordered Russia and other members of the former Soviet Union to countries further West. If a European Single Market is to mean anything at all, there will have to be a common immigration policy; and the only enforceable one will be that of the country with the lowest barriers.

The equalisation of the net return to workers of comparable skill and motivation is a prediction of classical economic theory. It was also a traditional goal of international socialism. I have no doubt that existing European workers will engage in extensive rearguard actions to stop these ideals from being realised. But in the long run, when not all of us will be dead, we may as well face the fact that there will be such tendencies at work. Maybe the growing disparities in the return to different kinds of skill and know-how will continue. But in addition there will be a tendency to the worldwide equalisation of returns for comparable work. Can anyone give a good ethical reason for objecting?

References

"The end of jobs for life", *The Economist*, 21 February 1998.

Chapter Eight
An Inflation Target Is Not Enough*

Fashions In Targets

Inflation targets are all the rage. The European Central Bank is almost certain to have a target both for a broadly based measure of the money supply and for inflation. But, if the record of the Bundesbank is anything to go by, the inflation target will in the last resort be the operational one and deviations of monetary growth will be explained away. A Bank of England study by Andrew Haldane hints that German monetary policy was "inflation targeting in all but name". New Zealand was the pioneer in adopting an inflation objective and has been joined by Canada, Finland and Sweden – to name only a few of the countries which have been most explicit on the matter. Britain has had such a target since the humiliating departure from the European Rate Mechanism by the Major Government in 1992; and several other countries have followed suit.

Responsibility for achieving an inflation objective – laid down originally at 2½ per cent per annum – was given to the Bank of England by the Blair Government in May 1997, when the Bank was made "operationally independent." The Governor of the Bank of England, Eddie George, repeatedly made it clear, as sterling shot up in the foreign exchange markets in 1996–97, that the Bank would continue to base monetary policy on the requirements of UK domestic price stability without an exchange rate target in mind, as the Bundesbank had always done. The specific feature of UK monetary policy since 1993 is that it is not based on current inflation, but on a forecast of inflation two years ahead.

Interestingly enough, the United States is one country which does not have a clear national commitment to steer monetary policy in the light of inflation alone. The US Federal Reserve is constrained by the Humphrey-Hawkins Act to take into account objectives such as growth and employment. There have been pressures from financial opinion for the Fed to massage its interpretation of the Act to mean low inflation alone. But the Fed could not get away with disclaiming responsibility for promoting the stability of the US, and even the world, economy. Alan Greenspan, the Fed chairman from the late 1980s, and no mean inflation fighter himself, has resolutely stood out against those who have tried to make inflation-fighting the sole objective of monetary policy. In

*Freshly compiled, drawing on *Financial Times* articles.

the winter of 1997–98 he made it clear that Fed policy was based, not only on US domestic considerations, but also on facts such as the collapse of the stock markets of the Asian "tigers" and the vulnerability of the Japanese banking system.

Weaknesses of Inflation Targets

Even if we could achieve a 2½ per cent inflation target, it would not meet reasonable sound money objectives, let alone anything wider. For it does not even aim at long-run price stability. Let us assume that the target could indeed be achieved. Then the value of money would halve over 28 years, that is over slightly more than one generation; and it would halve again in the generation after that. This would be true, even without the problem of base drift (which came to light earlier in the era of monetary targets). The point here is that a failure to achieve the inflation objective in any one year is not compensated, under an inflation target regime, by a shortfall in the following year, but forms the springboard for the next two years' targets.

There is a very strong case for saying that present inflation targets are in any case impractical. The two-year time horizon is both too short and too long. It is too long because it makes policy far too dependent on forecasts and downgrades current price data. It is too short because it can take far longer than two years for inflationary and deflationary trends to work themselves out. But when they do, the effects are much worse than the small percentage changes shown on conventional simulations.

The business cycle has been lengthening. The one which began in the trough of the 1981 recession lasted 11 years, compared with the four or five years typical of most of the postwar period. Similar remarks apply to prices. The inflation which peaked in 1990 had its roots, not just in the events of the preceding couple of years, but in the steady dribble of double digit annual percentage growth of credit and broad money over nearly a decade. The early and middle stages of that credit expansion were quite easily dismissed on technical grounds. In a notable address at Loughborough in 1986 by Robin Leigh-Pemberton, the then Governor of the Bank of England, the growth of credit and broad money was explained away as part of a shift by the public to holding greater liquid balances. Nor should the speech be ridiculed. It was a reasonable interpretation of the evidence at the time it was made. Unfortunately there were some signs that central bankers in many parts of the world were trying to compensate for past mistakes in an inflationary direction by erring in the 1990s on the side of severity. But that was as likely to be as successful as the habit of generals of fighting the last war.

Fallible Forecasts

There is no known way of forecasting inflation two years ahead let alone for the five- or ten-year period really needed to achieve reasonable price stability.

Forecasting equations rightly get changed in the light of events. In periods of unexpectedly low inflation they get rewritten in a more optimistic direction, and when inflation is unexpectedly high they are amended towards pessimism.

The trouble lies deeper than fallible forecasts. It lies in the pursuit of an unattainable ideal. In the heyday of stable money under the Gold Standard there were many years of five, six or seven per cent inflation. These were offset by other years when the price level actually dropped. The year-to-year variations actually had a function in coping with economic shocks. The attempt to achieve too fine a control may actually destabilise the economy.

The Austro-American economist Joseph Schumpeter horrified his contemporaries when – writing on the basis of pre-1914 experience – he claimed that inflation was inseparable from the process of economic growth. But he was no soft touch.[1] He emphasised that booms would be followed by corrective slumps, and he assumed that the world Gold Standard would ensure that the value of money was unlikely to be very different a couple of generations ahead. Indeed this is one way of interpreting Alan Greenspan's definition of "p inflation" as a state of affairs when the price level plays no major part business decisions.

The Pretence of Knowledge

How do central banks set about monitoring inflationary forces? I shall concentrate on the Bank of England, as it has been admirably explicit about its method of analysis. But most other central banks and official international monitoring organisations have similar methods of thinking. In the short to medium term, demand management, including monetary policy, has an effect on the real economy and also on the stability of financial institutions.

The prevailing model is illustrated by the chart. The Bank of England assumes that inflation is responsive to *ad hoc* cost pressures – such as import price changes – in the short run. But in the medium term, which is most important for monetary policy, it responds mainly to demand pressures as expressed by the "output gap".

The dotted line shows an estimate of the trend growth of output. Its position is also supposed to be compatible with a stable rate of inflation. So if you start with low inflation and move along the line, inflation will remain low. If output falls below trend, as in the early 1980s and early 1990s, there is an "output gap", which exercises downward pressure on inflation. If output is above trend, as in the late 1980s, there is said to be a "negative output gap" and inflation tends to increase. Add a few complications, such as expectational forces which are treated "off-model", and you have the theoretical basis of much policy thinking.

It is only fair to emphasise that I agree with the basic mechanism. Indeed I have over the years used such charts, both to indicate how monetary policy affects output and inflation, and also to show why it is not possible in the longer run to spend ourselves into desired rates of growth and employment. But while the model is useful for showing how the economy works, it is a mistake to try to use it too directly for policy purposes.

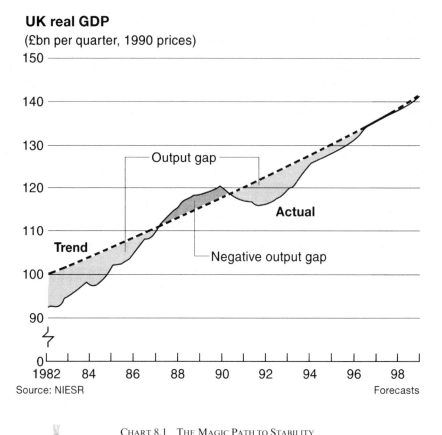

UK real GDP

(£bn per quarter, 1990 prices)

Source: NIESR

Forecasts

CHART 8.1   THE MAGIC PATH TO STABILITY

There are two great sources of ignorance in trying to apply it. The first is that we have very little idea what the trend growth of output is. Extrapolation from the past can go badly wrong. The official Treasury estimate has hovered around 2 to 2½ per cent per annum. The incoming Labour Chancellor, Gordon Brown, was first inclined, on taking office in 1997, to shade the estimate down, but afterwards to edge it up to take account of Labour's Welfare to Work plans. There are however critics who say that the official output figures understate the impact of information technology on productivity and who believe that the sustainable growth rate is a good deal higher than anything in the official range.

A less obvious, but even more important, uncertainty relates, not to the slope, but the position, of the trend line, and thus the size of the output gap. This gap does not literally measure how far an economy is from full physical utilisation of its resources. It aims to measure the distance from the equilibrium point at which there is sufficient spare capacity to prevent inflation accelerating or decelerating.

The same analysis could be presented in terms of equilibrium unemployment. Indeed it would be more honest, if politically more embarrassing, to do so. For while capacity can be adjusted reasonably quickly, changing the behaviour of labour markets is a much longer job. Some of us lost some of our friends for promoting Milton Friedman's idea of a "natural" rate of unemployment – subsequently labelled, less provocatively, the NAIRU (non-accelerating inflation rate of unemployment) – as a demonstration that governments could not spend their way into full employment. Now, in the sanitised and disguised form of the output gap, it is almost a universal orthodoxy.

Friedman has, however, consistently refused to offer his own estimate of either the NAIRU or the output gap because he believes that they are far too uncertain to be used as policy indicators. Not only are they uncertain: they are also liable to change. The Thatcher government's union-busting policies and the Blair government's Welfare to Work policies have both aimed to lower that rate so that we do not need so much unemployment to stop inflation from running away. And perhaps with some success. Both US and British unemployment fell for several years in the late 1990s well below the levels at which most model builders would have predicted a pay explosion.

Thus the Bank may not merely have been underestimating long-run growth trends. It may have been overestimating the amount of spare capacity or unemployment required to prevent an inflationary takeoff. Today's labour markets are far more competitive than they used to be. The US economy ran for several years in the 1990s above the supposed safe limits of operation without the feared inflation takeoff.

Above all, there is such a thing as a world deflationary or inflationary environment. When the environment is deflationary, relationships estimated from an inflationary past will no longer be reliable. Wage increases will fail to take off despite seemingly tight labour markets; and the rate of money supply growth consistent with stable prices will rise. How to combine recognition of such environmental changes with the intuition that inflation and deflation are monetary phenomena is an intellectual problem, touched on in the next chapter. But we cannot wait to resolve it before adjusting to new realities.

The Fed chairman, Alan Greenspan, frequently confounded the prophets by not raising interest rates despite the existence of a negative output gap in charts such as the one shown here. He was disinclined to move on the basis of forecasts and models and put more emphasis on whether or not he could see price increases in the pipeline.

Monetary Targets Not Superior

Critics have two questions to consider. First, is there a better way of approaching an inflation or a price level objective? Although this chapter is intended to express a sceptical case on inflation targets, it would in my view be a retrograde step to try to go back to a regime of monetary targets alone. The various monetary aggregates need to be watched. But not only have they in the past often moved in different directions; they have all at times proved distorted guides. Professor Gordon Pepper complains that monetarism – like Christianity – has never been tried. But if monetarism is defined in a non-sectarian way, not as a strict adherence to certain fallible monetary measures, but as an approach to inflation control through monetary policy rather than pay or price controls or fiscal fine-tuning, then it was not only tried but worked in Britain – with inevitable setbacks and lurches – throughout the 1980s and 1990s. (See Chart 2.2.)

Professor Milton Friedman, although he pioneered the revival of the monetary approach to inflation, was no longer advocating monetary growth targets by the mid-1990s. The reason may have been that he despaired of the world's central banks adopting what he regarded as the correct mechanism ("monetary base control") for operating such targets. Friedman's preference was for giving central banks a wide inflation target, ranging from say minus 3 to plus 3 per cent.[2] Translating this into the world of Gordon Brown and rounding upwards, this means 0 to 6 per cent. The reason for such a wide range is that it is unrealistic to expect year-to-year constancy of either inflation or real growth rates. Friedman would also prefer to judge the inflation prospect by the difference between the yield on conventional bonds and indexed ones. He understandably regards such financial market projections, on which individuals have staked their own money, as less prone to error than conventional econometric forecasts.

There is no perfect solution; but it would help to go more by actual evidence of inflation and less by forecasts and models, to accept that there are bound to be sizeable deviations from the neat slope shown on the right of Chart 8.1, and be content with being correct over an average of several years.

The Bank publishes one genuinely market-determined inflation forecast. This is based on the difference between the yield on nominal and index-linked gilt edged, which is also Friedman's latest preferred indicator. A Bank Working Paper by Breedon and Chada shows that even this series has over-predicted inflation in the past, perhaps due to the risk premium in gilt-edged yields. Should the Bank ruthlessly increase interest rates by as many percentage points as seem necessary to force the financial markets to lower inflation expectations in short order to 2½ per cent whenever they appear to be greater? Certainly not. It would probably not succeed even if it tried. For the result of such a draconian policy would on occasion be such a severe downturn in activity that the financial markets would rightly predict that policy-makers would be forced off the inflation target – as they were the Exchange Rate Mechanism – and make a U-turn instead.

The right moral is that in such circumstances the Bank should give the benefit of the doubt to tighter policy when it is unclear what to do, and thus hope gradually to persuade markets to take more seriously the official inflation objective. Even this sacred task would in an emergency have to take second place to the UK's duty, as a modest but significant member of the international financial community, to contribute to world financial stability.

A National Cash Objective

Rather than attempt to refine further the way in which inflation targets are pursued, we should ask: is there not a superior approach, which will take into account some of the other objectives of policy? Mainstream economists no longer believe that monetary or fiscal policy can "manage" demand and output in real terms. Attempts to do so, as we have painfully learned, can lead not merely to inflation but to accelerating inflation.

What demand management can however do is endeavour to maintain the growth of spending in nominal terms by an amount sufficient to sustain normal growth if costs and prices remain stable. It is unfortunate that "nominal demand" is such an off-putting phrase. The objective can be paraphrased as "a national cash objective". At a minimum, economic management should have the job of providing a safety net, that is of preventing a collapse of spending of the kind that occurred in the early 1930s. There is of course no way of guaranteeing a steady growth of spending of, say, 5 per cent, year in year out. I am not, however, talking about fine-tuning but of counteracting any pronounced upward or downward deviation from this rate over a period. (I have explained in more detail the crucial distinction between nominal and real demand in a previous work: Brittan, 1996).

An inflation target provides no such safety catch. If real output were to fall by 10per cent in a year and inflation remained at 1 to 2 per cent, everything would seem to be fine except for the blood on the streets. And less extreme situations in which output is stagnant or growing well below potential rates, but an inflation target is still not undershot, are all too possible. An example may have been Japan during the prolonged recession and stagnation of the 1990s.

National cash objectives can indeed be pursued by means of formal forecasts and with a heavy fine-tuning emphasis. But they can also be pursued in a way which puts less reliance on forecasting abilities and reduces the need for an econometric straitjacket. Indeed a nominal demand objective has one advantage not sufficiently stressed by its adherents. That is, it can enable us to rely less on forecasting ability. For it would not be disastrous if the best we could do would be to react to the current situation. We would simply look at how fast prices and output were rising. In a vigorous boom the real growth component would take Nominal GDP above the objective, even if inflation remains stable for a time. Thus the red light would shine for policy-makers. In a slump, policy would be loosened, so long as inflation had already been squeezed out, without the need to predict the turning point of the cycle or the speed with which "green shoots" might spread. Of course, if we can anticipate future changes in nominal demand growth, so much the better; but policy would not be impotent in the absence of such ability.

A nominal demand objective can be regarded as a compromise between an output and an inflation target. But it is a fairly subtle compromise. When spending threatens to rise too quickly, the counter-inflationary objective over-rides. If on the other hand output is sluggish and there is little or no inflation, then the output objective prevails. If inflation were, say, 2 per cent, but growth zero, interest rates would be reduced and perhaps other stimulatory measures taken. If output looked like growing by more than 5 per cent per annum, then policy would be tightened pre-emptively even if inflation were still low.

The best known measure of nominal demand is that called "Nominal GDP". This measure happens to be identical with MV: that is, the quantity of money (however defined) times its velocity of circulation. The idea is that a country's money managers should try to ensure that total spending rises at a rate consistent with non-inflationary growth. Some 5 per cent per annum would be within the ballpark for most western countries.

Interestingly enough a Nominal GDP objective would be more in the spirit of the original monetary targets than present policies. The original targets were based on the assumption that velocity was known within a relevant range. So a target for M, the money supply, was also a target for MV or Nominal GDP. This can also be written as PT, the price level times the volume of current transactions. So once a tight money policy had done its job of squeezing inflation, T would rise and output would automatically recover. With a purely price objective there is no such safety catch for output.

Many of the objections to a nominal demand objective misunderstand the proposal as one for substituting one short-term technocratic aim for another. But the way I see it is as an attempt to influence the climate rather than the weather. This makes delays and data revisions in nominal demand less important than critics suppose.

It is unfortunately necessary to make a few rather obvious clarifications. The expression "nominal GDP objective" is meant as a highbrow headline and not as the sole variable to monitor. It is difficult enough to get even the informed public to think in terms of a fresh concept. So that now that a few people know the slogan "nominal GDP", it is best to stick to it. In practice policy-makers would monitor a number of different measures of monetary demand just as they do at present of the inflation rate.

For the same reason that the Bank favours RPIY, an adjusted version of the Retail Prices Index, which excludes the effects of indirect tax changes as well as mortgage interest, it will be sensible to monitor expenditure at factor cost. Moreover some measure of domestic expenditure (which excludes the export component) might be more suitable than nominal GDP itself. One reason is that in UK conditions a domestic demand objective makes room for an improvement in the current balance of payments, if external demand rises, without making the balance of payments a policy objective. A connected reason is that domestic expenditure is more clearly under policy influence than that part of GDP which is determined by world conditions.

The most suitable level, however, at which to pursue a nominal demand objective at, would indeed be an international one, either the G7 or the EU or both. At these levels some of the measurement snags cancel each other out and Nominal GDP would be a reasonable approximation to what is required. More important: an international approach avoids the hubris of supposing that each country can stabilise business conditions on its own.

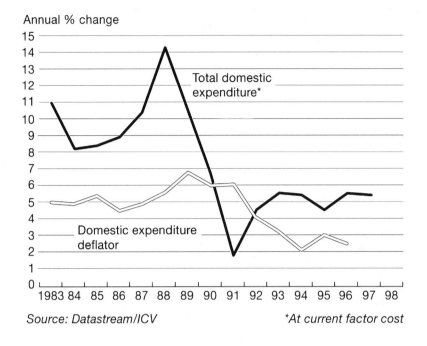

Source: Datastream/ICV   *At current factor cost

CHART 8.2 UK SPENDING AND INFLATION

A Bank Response

The Bank of England's Deputy Governor (and former economic director), Professor Mervyn King, has in fact defended the inflation target against some of the above criticisms in two lectures which deserve more attention than they have received.

In one given after the change of Government, he did something to defuse the worry about setting too narrow and rigid an inflation range on either side of the official 2½ per cent target. He freely admitted that what he calls "shocks" were likely to take inflation outside the official range. If inflation is pushed above the top of the target range – that is, above 3 per cent – after, say, a commodity price explosion, an attempt to return to the target range too quickly could lead to a severe loss of output and employment. The Bank would then have to decide whether to try to move back quickly to the target, or to move more slowly at the expense of temporarily higher inflation. The Deputy Governor is not only well aware that the Bank of England would have to explain such a departure from the inflation target in an open letter: he makes a positive virtue of the fact, remarking that the Monetary Policy Committee "will have many opportunities to restore the lost art of letter writing to British life".

I am not entirely happy about attributing all perverse movements to "shocks". I have already mentioned the possibility of an inflationary or deflationary atmosphere in which prices and pay do not observe previously estimated relationships. Then again, I wonder about the symmetry of the analysis. It may in practice prove difficult to get inflation, at least as estimated by conventional consumer price indices, to go much below 1 per cent even in a severe recession. So, looking at inflation alone might not reveal the need for, or the size of, a required policy relaxation. (All these objections could be put in terms of the uncertain position, instability or asymmetrical shape of the short-term Phillips curve. But this would be adding to the burden already placed on the less technical reader of this chapter without adding much of substance.)

It is a reasonable inference that King would have been happier with the original 1–4 per cent inflation target band proclaimed by Norman Lamont in 1992 than with the narrower range proclaimed by Gordon Brown five years later. In any case he is evidently trying to reduce the difference between the inflation target regime now officially in force and the nominal demand one preferred by some of the critics. This is all to the good. The way in which a regime is operated is at least as important as its official label. For all my reservations, the King analysis is several leagues ahead of the more common approach both in the "City" and in political circles – an approach which is to see any failure to stay within the 1½ to 3½ per cent inflation corridor around the 2½ per cent target as damaging.

And yet, and yet, and yet. Slogans and headline targets do matter. Friedman has for some time been worried that financial stability has relied too much on the acumen of specific individuals such as Alan Greenspan and Don Brash of the New Zealand Reserve Bank (or King in the UK). Relying on the hunch of one person, who will not always be there, and may not always retain his touch, is pretty hazardous. It is best to design monetary policy regimes (and political constitutions) which can be operated with a minimum of harm by more run of the mill individuals going by the conventional wisdom of the moment.

Towards Fuller Employment

I realise that this chapter may have been heavy going for the non-technical reader, even one who could be regarded as economically literate. On the other hand, it is not econometric or mathematical enough to fit in with current fashions of argument among professional monetary economists. But it would be sad indeed if the deficiencies of the author were to jeopardise the reception of the argument, which is indeed extremely important if we are to hope to return on a sustainable basis to something nearer to full employment. If we are to do so, wage behaviour will be crucial: both restraint at an aggregate level, and flexibility, including downward flexibility, at local, plant and occupational level.

A much rehearsed objection to such restraint and flexibility is that wages are a source of demand as well as of costs. If money wages are held back, will not purchasing power be curtailed as well, taking us roughly back to where we started in employment terms? This objection to pay flexibility was expressed by Keynes in the 1930s. It has been re-echoed by a well-known previous President of the EU Commission, Jacques Delors, and has at all times been voiced by union spokesmen.

It would be foolish to deny that such a self-stultifying chain of events could take place. A severe deflation in which wages and prices chase each other downwards in rapid succession would be as undesirable as the more familiar upward wage-price spiral. The best way out is, not to get lost in a taxonomic analysis of alternative reactions, but to make the policy suggestion that governments and central banks should be committed to maintaining a growth of demand in nominal terms – that is, achieving national cash objectives – low enough to prevent an inflationary take-off, but high enough to secure adequate growth when pay and prices are sufficiently restrained.

In other words, if pay moderation were to lead to a contraction in demand the authorities would be committed to compensate for this effect. Indeed the UK Medium Term Financial Strategy was sometimes presented in these terms in its heyday in the mid-1980s. Unfortunately there is no such assurance under the current regime. If you do not believe that policy should be a juggernaut set in motion by a few equations, then it is important to set at rest very reasonable public fears.

Professor James Meade used to say that macroeconomic management was the easier half of employment policy. All the more reason not to get it avoidably wrong.

References

Breedon, F. J., and Chada, J., (1997). *The Information Content of the Inflation Term Structure*. London: Bank of England Working Paper No 75.

Brittan S., (1995, 1996). *Capitalism with a Human Face*. Chapter 7. Cheltenham: Edward Elgar, 1995; London: Harper Collins 1996.

Haldane, A. G., (1997). *Some Issues in Inflation Targeting*. London: Bank of England Working Paper No 74.

King, M., (1994). *Monetary Policy in the UK*. London, The Institute for Fiscal Studies (Annual Lecture).

King, M., (1997). The inflation target five years on. *Quarterly Bulletin* (November) **97** (4), 934–992.

Pepper, G., (1997). *Inside Thatcher's Monetarist Revolution*. London: Institute of Economic Affairs.

PART III

LIVING WITH PARTIAL KNOWLEDGE

Chapter Nine
Causation In Economic Affairs*

Introduction

An invitation to give an address with "David Hume" in its title is enormously flattering and also, frankly, more than a little daunting. Clearly I should make David Hume himself my starting point. I have always found his thought appealing; and the appeal has grown as I have tried to move from headline knowledge to slightly more detailed examination. His scepticism and iconoclasm led to a profound belief in toleration, unusual in his own time and only superficially accepted in our own. He directed his iconoclasm towards revolutionary as well as conventional thinkers. In today's parlance, he was an individualist rather than a communitarian; and he had no truck with the church-and-state pieties of his arch antagonist, Samuel Johnson.

Of course, being human, there were some missing elements in his make-up. He lacked that passionate indignation at injustice and oppression, found in his contemporary Voltaire, who was very similar in outlook but much his inferior as a philosopher. But we should value thinkers for what they have given us rather than bemoan what lay outside their range.

Hume's few essays on political economy are as apt and as controversial today as when they were when originally published in the middle of the eighteenth century. He struck a very modern note in observing that all calculations concerning the balance of trade "are founded on very uncertain facts and suppositions". He exposed the nonsensical fears which statesmen had "with regard to the balance of trade and the fear that gold and silver may be leaving them". Indeed a Yorkshireman (or a Scot) might have had similar "melancholy reflections" on the imbalance which probably then existed in transactions with London, "did not long experience make people easy on this head".

Yet these essays and his more massive *History of England* were written almost by way of relaxation. His reputation rests on his philosophy, in particular his *Treatise of Human Nature* and his *Enquiry Concerning Human*

* A revised version of the Presidential Address to The David Hume Institute, delivered on 31 October, 1996. I am indebted to Ken Binmore, Clive Crook, Helena Cronin, Mervyn King, Nigel Lawson, Patrick Minford and David Willetts for their comments on earlier drafts.

Understanding, which established his position as the greatest of British philosophers.

Hume's purpose was clearly stated in his own Introduction to the *Treatise*. It was to approach unresolved questions by examining the principles of human nature and to do so by "the application of experimental philosophy to moral subjects". The unifying feature of his work in pure philosophy and in subjects like political economy was his assumption that the data were already well known to a reasonably educated person and that what was required was "a cautious observation of human life as it appears in the common course of the world, by men's behaviour in company, in affairs and in their pleasures" – and not hesitating to use careful introspection to provide some of his data.

Causation

I knew all along that I could not acquire an adequate understanding of Hume's more abstract writings in the time available to me. But it would be cowardly to duck all the issues raised. So I sought a compromise. In an anonymous Abstract at the end of the *Treatise*, almost certainly written by Hume himself (as Keynes discovered with the aid of Sraffa), the author gives the analysis of "causation" as the main innovation of the work. So my decision was to try to illustrate some of the problems of causation by modern economic examples.

I intend to give the plot away right now. My theme is that the search for causes has only limited value in pursuing many of the bigger questions of legitimate public interest. Because I have thrown doubt on the usefulness of insisting on the search for causes of complex human phenomena, I have been understood to be jettisoning the whole concept of cause-and-effect and thus undermining the very foundation of rational thought. Not so. My own topic – the problematic nature of causation in the social sciences – is not the same as Hume's problem, which was the justification of causal reasoning in general. But I can claim to be following in the spirit, although not the letter, of Hume, who was concerned to debunk the idea that there was some profound mystery about causation which would provide the key to human wisdom.

Hume's starting point was the lack of any necessary link between what is regarded as a cause and its effect. In a key passage of the *Treatise* he wrote: "Suppose two objects are to be presented to us, of which the one is the cause and the other the effect; 'tis plain, that from the simple consideration of one, or both these objects we shall never perceive the tie by which they are united or be able to pronounce that there is a connection between them".[1] This was of course linked to his well-known doubts about induction: what warrant do we have for assuming that a generalisation based on past data will hold in the future? As a modern philosopher puts it, "The dispute between Humeans and non-Humeans on causality is fundamentally on whether there is more to causality than regularity of succession" (O'Hear, 1985).

We can avoid knocking our heads against the problem of induction by looking at Hume's positive account of what people usually mean when they say "A causes B". For him the key to causation is "constant conjunction". He added the further condition that the effect has to follow the cause – or as his modern followers would say, must not come before it. This amendment has been made to allow for connections between simultaneous events,[2] but in practice Hume's simple version will often do.

Writers of elementary books on logical fallacies and of statistical texts are fond of warning us of two fallacies:- (a) confusing causality with correlation and (b) of *post hoc ergo propter hoc*, that is of saying that because B followed A it was caused by A. Such guidebooks rarely tell us, however, what causality does mean.

Hume himself comes very near to saying that if the correlation is perfect and the sequence invariable then A indeed causes B. Hume also introduced a third element, contiguity in space and time. But this is not helpful, as it makes it difficult to account for action at a distance and has been dropped by sympathetic modern commentators such as Ayer. The basic Humean position may thus be restated: If A is always followed by B, and B never occurs without A, then A causes B. This is in line with Hume's general conclusion, foreshadowed in the Introduction to the *Treatise*, that no ultimate justification can be given for the general principles of human reasoning. He believed that it was habit that led people to expect like causes to produce like effects. As I understand it, Kant went further by treating causation as one of the categories which human beings inescapably use to understand the world. As a modern cognitive scientist might put it, we are just "wired up" to make certain connections.

There is of course a large modern philosophical literature on causation, on which I claim no expertise. John Stuart Mill tried to formalise the notion of multi-causality by saying that in such cases all contributory causes must be individually necessary for an event to occur; and in their totality they must be both necessary and sufficient. In the twentieth century the notion of causality has been extended from certainty to statistical likelihood (now known as the "inductive statistical" or "statistical relevance" model). Where the law in question is of a statistical kind, the initial conditions increase the probability of an event to be examined. This is in line with the Granger concept of causality in econometrics, which states that X causes Y if the prediction of the current value of Y is enhanced by using past predictions from X.[3] Some writers prefer to regard statistical relevance as a different concept rather than a special case of causality. The issue is mainly verbal.

Then there is the question of negative causation. Is the failure of a sailor to close the safety hatch to be regarded as a cause of a ferry sinking? Is the failure of the Federal Reserve or the Bank of England to act appropriately to be regarded as the cause of a particular inflation or recession? Here again we have a choice of usage. Words such as cause do not have intrinsic meanings; and it is a matter of convenience how far we extend their usage to cover complex instances or puzzles or new developments.

The most important modern innovation is the emphasis on the covering law. This is often attributed to G F Hempel. But my own illustration is adapted from Karl Popper (1974). A causal explanation of an event, according to this model, is its derivation from a universal law together with certain initial conditions. Consider a copper thread from which a weight is suspended. The universal law states that every such thread is characterised by a given tensile strength; and whenever a thread is loaded with a weight exceeding that which characterises the tensile strength of the thread, it will then break. In addition there are the initial conditions which apply to the particular event. One is that the tensile strength of this thread is, for instance, one pound. The other is that the thread is loaded with a weight of two pounds. From the combination of the universal law and the initial conditions we deduce that the thread will break. As Popper would have been the first to stress, the universal law cited here is pretty primitive. Many scientists would not be happy until they had deduced this law from some general encompassing theoretical system such as Newton's Laws of Motion.

What advantages are there from encompassing theories? The aesthetic one is not to be despised. It is more satisfying to deduce many lower level laws from a few general principles rather than treat them as *ad hoc* regularities. If this can be done, we are likely to feel that we have done more to explain the phenomena. But such general theories ought also to provide better predictions if we are to have much real confidence in them. There is, however, no guarantee that the desired general theories can be found in all spheres. We might have to be content with lower level theories such as the posited breaking point for copper wire – or even with the simple regularities such as those that Hume himself identified, covering the impact of one billiard ball on another.

The situation in political economy is that we know both the tensile strength and the weights placed on the thread only within very wide margins of error. In addition the tensile strength can change over time. Even in our physical example rust can have such an effect. The background conditions under which the causal relationship between the load weights and the wire apply are obvious and trivial: the weights must be accurate; the observations honestly reported; there must not be a howling gale in the laboratory, and so on.

Such background factors are normally assumed away in physical science under the slogan "other things being equal" (*ceteris paribus*). But other things in economics (and the other social sciences) may be of enormous importance. The whole "Lucas Critique" of conventional econometric models is based on their failure to take adequately into account changes in policy regimes.

But to throw up our hands in despair, as philosophers who dislike social science sometimes do, is quite wrong. We know in the copper thread example, that events are not completely random; and despite all the complications of rust, atmospheric conditions, measurement error and so on, a sufficiently large weight will break a sufficiently thin thread. Similarly in political economy we know that if a sufficient amount of spending power is injected into the economy by the government or central banks, eventually inflation will increase even if we cannot state the principle as precisely as we can in the copper thread example.

Whatever may happen in the remoter areas of physics, Hume's concept of causation as regularity plus succession still has a lot going for it. Many of the examples given to ridicule it merely suggest that sufficient instances have not been examined covering a sufficient variety of contexts. Sometimes the causal hypothesis is just distorted to raise a cheap laugh. For instance, it is said that the sending of Christmas cards does not cause Christmas to occur. Of course it does not. It is the prospect of Christmas in the minds of millions which precedes the sending of cards – and one may say is a cause of their despatch.

The primitive hypothesis about the sending of cards causing Christmas can be easily falsified. I write for an organisation which has decided not to send Christmas cards. Even if its practice were copied throughout the length and breadth of the land, Christmas will still occur. The testing of the more sophisticatcd hypothesis about the prospect of Christmas would require more recondite experiments, e.g. the successful propagation of a false report that the impact of a comet would destroy life on earth before 25 December next.

Human Affairs

Why then is it so difficult to find simple chains of cause and effect in human societies? When I started preparing this lecture I accepted too unreflectively the conventional view that it is the human factor that makes it difficult to find reliable causal laws in the social sciences. But I am now inclined to place more responsibility on the feature of complexity – the interaction of many forces, which also makes it difficult to attribute ultimate causes to physical phenomena, such as earthquakes or thunderstorms, let alone climatic change.

Indeed, the human factor makes it slightly easier to proceed in the social sciences. For it is, at least, possible to get a lead by asking people questions about their motives, or relying on what they have put on record, or what we know from simple observation or from works of literature. Indeed, it is common in economic theory to start with simple introspection, as Hume did himself. There can be no objection to this method so long as its results can be empirically tested in some form.

The basic reason why simple causation is difficult to apply to human affairs is that the latter are complex phenomena. The American philosopher, Bernard Lewis, has illustrated the problem in relation to a road crash. If someone says that a flat tyre was the cause, another the driver's drunkenness and yet another the upbringing, which made him so reckless, I do not think any of them disagree that the causal history includes all three. They may disagree about which part of the cause or history is important for a particular inquiry. They may be looking for the most remarkable, the most remediable or the most blameworthy part. Events such as road accidents or ferry sinkings have in common that they are affected by a multiplicity of influences, any one of which can be regarded as the basic cause, depending on the point of view of the inquirer. If an investigation of a ferry crash shows that someone forgot to pull down the safety hatch but that other conditions, such as weather, load, and so on, were normal, it is natural to regard the failure to observe the elementary safety precaution as the principal cause of the accident. But as actual reports on such disasters demonstrate, such simple cases are rare. Normally a multiplicity of factors is involved.

A tribunal concerned with guilt or liability for damages may point the finger at the negligence of responsible personnel. A parliamentary inquiry may look for changes in public policy which might reduce the frequency of such accidents in the future, even in the face of human error, such as putting more resources into road design or lifeboat-launching systems. A moralist might point to a business climate in which the bottom line takes precedence over measures to safeguard human lives. An ambitious sociologist might want to chart changes in attitude to risk. There is no end to the number of points of view from which the search for ultimate causes might emanate. No wonder the historian, James Joll, prefaces his book, *The Origins of the First World War*, with a quotation from the end of Act II of Wagner's *Tristan and Isolde*:-

> *King Mark*: Who will make known to the world the inscrutably deep secret cause?
> *Tristan*: That, King, I cannot tell you; and what you ask, that you will never learn.

It does not really help to replace the search for a single cause by the search for several causes. First of all, as we see from examples ranging from the hypothetical car accident to the origins of the First World War, the number of causes is indefinitely large. It is only helpful to list them if some order of relative importance can be given, or at least if they can be placed in some sort of hierarchy. But the task is made more difficult, as I have tried to show, by the multiplicity of points of view from which an event, or class of events, can be viewed.

Friedmanism

In applying these ideas to economics, I have found it helpful to look at the monetary work of Milton Friedman. Yet I discovered, from circulating earlier drafts of this lecture that, so great is the prejudice against him in some British circles, that the critical use of his ideas merely as an illustration turned some people off. One reason why I have nevertheless chosen them as a jumping off ground is because of the thirty-year old argument on whether he had confused correlation with causality. Another reason is that an American author, J D Hammond, has written a study devoted exclusively to *Causality Issues in Friedman's Economics*, from which I learned a great deal. I was also impressed by Friedman's own remark that he avoided in his scientific work the word "cause", which he believes to be a very tricky concept.

Friedman's best known proposition is that an increase in the quantity of money above the rate at which output can rise is a necessary and sufficient condition for a takeoff in nominal demand and therefore of inflation. Conversely, a substantial decline in the quantity of money is a necessary and sufficient condition for the collapse of demand which occurs in a depression. He accepts that over the short term and in mild fluctuations, there can be mutual interaction between money and nominal demand; but in longer run changes or in large fluctuations, he believes money to be the senior partner.[4]

Throughout his career, Milton Friedman has been attacked by critics saying that his ideas are based on a mere association between money and prices (or money and Nominal GDP). The critics have asserted that there could easily have been a common cause at work or that money responded passively to economic movements, accommodating whatever change had occurred. Friedman was of course aware of these traps. Indeed he went out of his way to look for a great variety of evidence, ranging from comparisons between different countries with different institutions, to detailed accounts of how the Federal Reserve decided policy and fairly simple econometric tests designed to show whether specific events could have been better predicted from "Keynesian" variables, such as investment or government spending, or from the behaviour of the money stock. The real problems with Friedman's eclectic approach is that it takes a lifetime's work to assemble and half a lifetime to assess critically. Most people will have to take something on trust.

We can ask about the magnitude and the stability of the relationship. We can ask for a working definition of money and investigate how robust it is in the face of financial innovation. We can ask how useful the proposition is if the time lags are "long and variable". We can ask how robust it is in the face of "Goodhart's Law" that economic relationships break down when used for policy purposes.[5] We can also ask for a more detailed specification of the assumed background conditions. Does the money-price relationship hold in the face of a depression with large unemployed resources? And how far can we then go in injecting money before the simple money-price relationship takes hold again? It is for such reasons that I would part company from the technical monetarists and relate inflation and economic fluctuations to "nominal demand" (cash spending in the economy), which often has a monetary origin but cannot always be related by formula to movements in some specified definition of money.

But there is another type of criticism.[6] Friedman has been criticised for substituting mere empirical correlations for fundamental explanations. But what would a fundamental explanation look like? The demand for something more fundamental might mean that we would like a more reductionist attempt to explain macro-economic behaviour in terms of more widely accepted hypotheses about human conduct. But suppose we succeed in doing so? Many monetarists have indeed tried to ground their hypotheses in the rational allocation of wealth between money and other assets by utility maximising individuals. We have still not escaped empirical regularities. For it is an empirical matter whether or not, or to what extent, human beings obey what economists regard as the principles of rational self-interested conduct. To take an example from a different area: many people will follow economic logic and not bother to vote if the cost to them is heavy, e.g. a long walk in pouring rain, or missing a favourite television programme. But they will vote if the cost is relatively trivial, e.g. a short car journey to the polling booth.

Friedman freely admits that his monetary propositions are only the beginning of an answer to the sources or cures of inflation or deflation. Excess money may be injected into an economy for all sorts of reasons: gold discoveries, financial innovations, governments trying to spend more than they can finance; misguided full employment policies, or numerous other possible sources. The chain of events will not be the same on all occasions.

The futility of the search for a single true cause or even a list of causes, of a particular event, is particularly clear in relation to the Great Depression of the inter-war years. No-one claims to have a complete explanation. The post-First World War gold standard was prone to deflationary disturbances. The US financial system was fragile. The Federal Reserve failed to prevent a multiple monetary contraction when it could still have done so. The premature death of its outstanding leader, Benjamin Strong, made Federal Reserve failure more likely. But having discussed these and many other factors, such as the Wall Street boom and bust, what is gained by seeking something called "the cause"? Friedman supporters insist that he has never attempted a complete explanation either of business fluctuations or of the Great Depression, but concentrated on the way that bad monetary policy has made them worse.

A Simple Demand-Pull Model

It may be helpful at this stage to outline a fairly mainstream demand-pull model of inflation and deflation, but one which is both simpler and more encompassing than that usually presented. A necessary condition for sustainable growth without inflation is that nominal demand should be rising at a moderate pace. For an advanced western country this rate is unlikely to differ very much from 5 per cent per annum, but nothing hangs on this estimate.

If nominal demand increases more quickly for any length of time we can expect inflation. If it rises more slowly or actually declines we can expect deflation, that is falling prices. There will be some temporary acceleration of output in the first case before the whole impact is dissipated in rising prices. As Hume himself said: "Money, when increasing, gives encouragement to industry during the interval between the increase in money and the rise of prices". In the second case there will be some fall in output and employment, before pay and prices become adjusted to falling prices and before long-term contracts can be adjusted.

The two real economy effects are not necessarily symmetrical. Because of various resistances and rigidities, you might require a large and long lasting slump in output to accommodate to a regime of falling prices. This fall may be greater than the temporary boost to output on the upside before inflation develops. In both cases the details depend on the development of expectations, on which there are few reliable rules.

Does this mean that changes in the growth of nominal demand are the "causes" of slumps and inflationary booms? We need to go slowly at this point. For we can extend the inquiry forward or backward. If we extend it forward, we can trace the way an excessive flow of demand reduces spare capacity, lowers unemployment and increases unfilled vacancies – in modern parlance reduces the so-called "output gap". This in turn brings upward pressure to bear on wages and prices. Thus many analysts now choose to examine inflationary and deflationary pressures in terms of the output gap.

Alternatively we can move backwards and ask what lies behind changes in the growth of nominal demand. Friedman follows Hume in singling out monetary changes.

I would liken the chain of events to an upside down funnel with a constriction in the middle. Rapid or deficient monetary growth may originate from many different sources. And the channels by which monetary changes go through first to nominal demand and then to prices may also vary. One justification (although it is not Friedman's main one) for picking on the monetary constriction would be the belief that this is where policy can most easily get a handle. For any error in diagnosing more fundament influences will show itself in variations in the flow of money through the constriction. On the Friedman analysis, by acting here national authorities can prevent the worst inflationary and deflationary excesses, whatever their ultimate sources and whatever the exact way in which they fan out.

There are, as already mentioned, many arguments about how to measure money and how much its relationship to nominal demand fluctuates. Partly for this reason, I would locate the constriction in the funnel at which policy can best operate at a slightly later stage than Friedman does – in corrections to nominal demand when that is seen to be increasing too quickly or too slowly. Also, focusing on nominal demand allows one to take account of non-monetary forces such as fiscal policy or stock exchange panics (which, in monetarist language, affect velocity).

The weakest part of the model just sketched relates to the institutional forces – including public attitudes and beliefs – which have been making for a less inflationary environment in a large part of the 1990s. Some sea-changes may well have been taking place. Increases in the money supply or in the demand for labour, which previously might have touched-off a wage-price spiral, do not seem to have done so in some recent periods. One can concede this much without endorsing the "inflation is over" school of thought, about which it is far too early to be sure. Meanwhile, like most analysts, I have to fall back on changes in the parameters which link monetary and other changes to inflation. This is a limp procedure but there is no guarantee that anyone will find a better way.

There is one negative conclusion that I would draw from these difficulties. This is that from the point of view of diagnosis and policy, insight and flair are more important than the school of thought to which an analyst belongs, for instance whether he or she claims to be a monetarist, a Keynesian, an institutionalist or a post-Marxist.

Speaking as an upholder of a broadly monetary approach to inflation, I would still find that the analysis of a sensible institutionalist who realises that monetary policy has a role in accommodating or resisting the forces he describes, could prove more illumination today than a rigid monetarist who applies parametric estimates from past data without asking how far they still apply. Such a monetarist would be like a metallurgist who waits for so long for overwhelming evidence that the tensile strength of a wire has changed through rusting that meanwhile the weight has dropped on his foot.

Modes of Explanation

The moral may be that wide-ranging causal explanations are out of place in political economy or the social sciences generally. It is sometimes possible to locate conclusively proximate causes of a particular event – for instance an assassin's bullet was the cause of the death of the Austro-Hungarian archduke in 1914 in Sarajevo. But as soon as we look for more ultimate causes we run into the quagmire of the search of the causes of World War One.

What is the best way to proceed in analysing large scale human events where simple cause and effect relations are unlikely to be satisfactory?

As so often it is easier to see what not to do. There is one cop-out which often goes by the name of post-modernism. There may be reasonable interpretations of this notion. But a recent paper by RAW Rhodes summarises the post-modern critique in the following way.

1. There is no adequate means for representing external reality.

2. There are no real world objects of study other than those inherent within the mental make-up of persons.

3. All knowledge claims are intelligible and debatable only within particular interpretive communities.

4. Truth is just a language game and reality a linguistic convention.

There is a nugget of truth in all these claims. But they are a recipe for disaster if adopted by historians, sociologists, economists and policy analysts. The doubts expressed are entirely legitimate and need to be analysed when discussing epistemology – the nature of knowledge and our claims to it. But when we pass to the social sciences or to discussions of policy, we have to assume that there is an external reality, which we are not free to invent as we like. Indeed the greatest sceptic of all, David Hume, was most insistent that when he went into company and discussed the world and its concerns he put his sceptical doubts behind him.

The need is for some approaches which recognise the near impossibility of a value-free social science or history and the inevitable injection of personal points of view, and yet insists on some reality check. For the time being, at least, we need to follow more informal approaches to the different schools of thought which try to explain large scale economic events. There are at least four key ideas that need mentioning: paradigm, research programme, story and historical interpretation.

Thomas Kuhn, the science historian, made great play with the notion of a paradigm, a framework not normally open to refutation and in which all subordinate theories have to be placed. One example in economics would be neo-classical market-clearing. Another might be sticky wages in more Keynesian models. Counter-evidence is explained away. Eventually one paradigm replaces another by a process which, in Kuhn's view, need be "neither rational nor ultimately correct". It will do so when it captures the "hearts and minds" of commanding figures of the scientific community. This picture may be exaggerated or unfair with regard to the physical sciences, but it applies all too well in the way in which fashions such as Keynesian demand management, monetarism or neo-classical market-clearing succeed each other in political economy.

The Hungarian-British philosopher Imre Lakatos put forward the more positive idea of "research programmes". The idea here is that a series of theories have to be assessed in common. They are welded together by series of methodological do's and don'ts. Research programmes are not overthrown by simple decisive tests. Instead they become either "progressive", when they are fruitful in producing new knowledge, or stagnationary if they produce mainly *post hoc* explanations of what we already knew. (The investigation of properties of alternative monetary regimes may be regarded a research programme.) Lakatos was unusually tolerant for a philosopher of science, saying: "We should be modest about our projects because rival programmes may eventually triumph". And "a programme now doing badly may eventually recover its momentum".

Both paradigms and research programmes are responses to the difficulty of finding conclusive falsification even of physical theories. The main difference is that the paradigm approach is more cynical and stresses turf battles between scientists and the role of institutions and conventional opinion in conferring victory. The research programme approach tries to show how science can advance, and evidence be taken into account, even in the absence of conclusive tests.

Of the two I prefer the research programme. More negative philosophers of science – such as Kuhn – make their task unnecessarily difficult by deliberately ignoring technological applications as intellectually beneath their attention. But surely the Hiroshima bomb or the launching of Cape Canaveral satellites shows that the physics behind them represents more than the triumph of particular models in the politics of the scientific establishment?

Much the most explosive of the explanatory notions is that of *stories*, occasionally called narratives. I have heard "What's your story?" asked by exasperated members of seminars who have wanted to know what the speaker really believes happens in the world. I had thought of stories as relatively informal accounts either of a single event or of a whole class of events. For instance, the received account of the role of Winston Churchill's return to gold in 1925 in worsening inter-war unemployment is quite a good story. There are however other stories. A more general type of story relates to the role of the entrepreneur who supplies, not capital or managerial skills, but imagination in seeing possibilities that most people have missed. The crucial difference is surely between an informed story and the recital of whatever fancies or prejudices come into one's head. Some people, however, associate stories and narratives with the slogans of post-modernism and detect in them a sign of opposition to science in general and Darwinism in particular.

These contradictory and explosive reactions reinforce my own sympathy for the fourth category which derives from Popper, not as an analyst of hard science, but in his role as a historical and sociological critic. Here he talks of *historical interpretations* which are inescapable and can be illuminating. These interpretations will embody a short chain of cause and effect relationships, which need not be trivial; but they are not causal theories themselves. Thus a conclusive choice cannot be made between them. At most one can say that some interpretations turn out to be more fruitful than others. The notion seems to encompass most of what is useful in "stories", without all the smoke and dust.

For instance, an account of the origins of the First World War in terms of Anglo-German naval rivalry is inevitably partial and one-sided. But as far as it goes it must be consistent with known evidence and if possible have links with other interpretations such as the Alliance system and the absence of any preventive system akin to the modern hot line.

An interesting application is to the fall of the Roman republic. Conventional histories explain the particular sequence of events by which Julius Caesar rather than Pompey became master of Rome with the normal combination of luck and judgment. But, as Garry Runciman rightly remarks, the deeper question is: what were the conditions which made the survival of an agricultural aristocratic republic unlikely and the emergence of personal rule abetted by a large bureaucracy highly probable?. In telling his version of the story, Runciman implicitly makes use of a large number of predictive laws of an "If . . . then . . ." variety. They concern for instance the threshold size of empire beyond which an ancient republic could not cope. It would be interesting to have these propositions explicitly set out, even if they could only be done in terms of probabilities. And one would like to know how far these rules still apply and how far they have to be modified in the light of modern conditions.

It may, however, be that any such attempt at formal rules would turn out to be pedantic, trivial or too heavily qualified to be worthwhile. In that case we are back with Popper's historical interpretation. There is nothing wrong with that; but it differs from science in that at least some alternative interpretations can live side by side, with no decisive way of choosing between them.

Policy

When it comes to public policy we cannot of course just contemplate different kinds of interpretation at our leisure. Nor can we rely on there being individuals of insight and flair either being available or being in in key positions. How then should we proceed?

Unfortunately I cannot give a general answer to this question. The present tendency is to bypass insoluble theoretical problems with institutional processes. An example is the fashion for central bank independence. The trend is to lay down an objective and leave the central banks discretion in its pursuit. There is an analogy here with the law courts which are bound by the laws of the land but are allowed discretion in interpreting and enforcing them. The idea, when sensibly stated, is not, to leave central banks as freely floating bodies able to do exactly what they like. It is for operational independence in following a politically determined goal.

What should this objective be? Inflation targets have been adopted because of the failure of attempts to steer the economy by what is known as intermediate objectives such as the money supply or the exchange rate. My own view is that inflation targets will not in the end prove adequate. For, among other things it says nothing about what can be done to avoid recessions and excessive fluctuations in the real economy with which in practice every central bank, including the Bundesbank, has been concerned. My own preference, already outlined in Chapter Eight, is for an objective for nominal demand. This is a very off-putting term. But it basically means monitoring the flow of cash spending in an economy, which needs to grow at a moderate pace to leave room for some growth but without financing inflation.

The relevance to the causation argument comes when one considers why such objectives, which command by now quite a bit of high quality support in several countries, have not yet caught on. The official reason given by most economists is that estimates for Nominal GDP or alternative measures come in late and are subject to much revision. This objection comes from people who cannot envisage general guidelines without precise targets at which to shoot.

But I do not think that this is the main reason why say, younger research economists do not find the notion attractive. Here we do come back to the harm caused by an obsessive search for causes. For if you have a nominal demand target you accept that spending in the economy may be rising too quickly or falling for a great variety of reasons on different occasions. You accept this fact and try to find ways of curbing or boosting spending as the case may be.

But this very acceptance of events as they come deprives such a guideline of some of its intellectual interest. For researchers like to delve into the causes of phenomena and not just examine the cures or palliatives which may be possible when they occur. Suppose that the authorities need to curb inflation. Most economists believe that there is still a short-term Phillips curve. In other words if you want to reduce inflation, you have to pay a price in temporary unemployment. What the contemporary researcher would like to know how big the price is – in other words how much extra unemployment you need and for how long for a given reduction in inflation. Having made a stab at this he or he can ask the government what its reaction function is.

My proposal would indeed be unnecessary if there were a fully specified and reliable short term Phillips curve and if this could be explained to the government of the day. But the truth is that there is no such animal. The trade-off between unemployment and inflation varies with time and place and according to prevailing expectations, the structure of wage-setting institutions, the international environment and vaguer but more still important matters such as the climate of opinion. It also depends on the skill with which the policy is implemented and explained. A nominal demand approach, on the other hand, faces up to these limitations on our ability to predict precise paths and accepts a more general objective which will merely try to curb unnecessary deep recessions and also any takeoff into inflation.

I bring this example up again to show that you do not have to retreat into mysticism, or into dictators hearing voices from heaven, simply because the causal chains in human are too complex to lay down in a mechanical way.

Appendix

Bertrand Russell maintained that causal statements did not have the importance normally attributed to them even in the physical sciences. He remarked in his now under-rated *History of Western Philosophy*: "Propositions of the form 'A causes B', where A and B are classes of events, do not occur in well-developed scientific theories". This quotation has caused some puzzlement. What could Russell have meant by his assertion, which he threw out casually in the course of his chapter on David Hume? As it is quite impossible to ask him (unless his theological views were totally wrong!), let me try to reconstruct his argument as best I can.

He could have meant the following:

(a)   It is usual in advanced physical science to think of mutually determining systems like the solar system, where it makes no sense to ask what is the cause of the earth going round the sun. Talk of causality is even more misplaced in Einstein's General Relativity, where the motion of heavenly bodies derives from the geometrical properties of space-time. It also makes no sense to ask about cause and effect in general equilibrium Walrasian economics. The prices and quantities are all mutually determining and there is no causal arrow from one to another.

(b)   Causal relationships may apply to lower grade events, such as lightning or thunderstorms. Above all, causality is used in the natural sciences to explain individual events. The answer to why the apple fell to the ground is not "gravity" but because a boy shook a branch of the tree. I have argued that even individual causality will only take us a certain way in the less well-developed social sciences.

The reasons for the limitations of causal reasoning in economics are more mundane than the ones Russell mentions. They rest on the very great importance of background conditions – which dwarf in importance such causal laws as can be found – and the extreme multi-causality of most events.

References

Ayer, A. J., (1980). *Hume*. London: Fontana.
Ayer, A. J., (1982). *Philosophy in the 20th Century*. London: Unwin Paperback.
Basu, K., (1981). Causality and economic theory. *Indian Economic Review*, pp 274–285.
Blaug, M., (1992). *The Methodology of Economics*. 2nd edn. Cambridge: University Press.
Bootle, R., (1996). *The End of Inflation*. London: N Brearley.
Friedman, M., (1992). *Monetary Mischief – Episodes in Monetary History*. New York, Harcourt Brace.
Friedman, M., and Schwartz, A., (1963). *A Monetary History of the United States, 1857–1960*. Princeton: University Press.

Hammond, J. D., (1995). *Theory and Measurement: Causality Issues in Milton Friedman's Monetary Economics.* Cambridge, Mass: MIT Press.

Hausman, D., (ed) (1992). *Economics and Philosophy.* 2nd edn. New York:

Hempel, G. F., (1993). Explanation in science and history. In Ruben, D (ed), *Explanation.* Oxford: Oxford University Press.

Hicks, J. R., (1979). *Causality in Economics.* Oxford: Blackwell.

Hume, D.,(1741–2). Of the balance of trade. In *Essays, Moral, Political and Literary.* Modern edn, 1985. Indianapolis: Liberty Classics,

Hume, D., (1777). *Inquiries Concerning the Human Understanding and Concerning the Principles of Morals.* Modern edn, 1966. Oxford: Clarendon Press.

Hume, D., (1740). *A Treatise of Human Nature.* Modern edn, 1978. Oxford: Clarendon Press. (*NB: this edition contains the Abstract. Not all others do*).

Kennedy, P., (1992). *A Guide to Econometrics.* 3rd edn. Oxford: Blackwell.

Kuhn, T. S., (1970). *The Structure of Scientific Revolutions.* 2nd edn. Chicago: University of Chicago Press.

Lakatos, I., and Musgrave, A., (eds), (1970). *Criticism and the Growth of Knowledge.* Cambridge: University Press,

Mill, J. S., (1843). *A System of Logic.* London:

O'Hear, A., (1985). *What Philosophy Is.* London: Penguin.

O'Hear, A., (1989). *An Introduction to the Philosophy of Science.* Oxford: Oxford University Press.

Popper, K. R., (1974). *The Logic of Scientific Discovery.* London: Hutchinson.

Popper, K. R., (1969). *The Poverty of Historicism.* London, Routledge.

Rhodes, R. A. W., (1997). *Organising Perspectives on British Government.* Department of Politics, University of Newcastle-upon-Tyne.

Runciman, W. G., (1998). *The Social Animal.* London: HarperCollins.

Russell, B., (1946). *A History of Western Philosophy.* London: Unwin.

Chapter Ten
The Many Failings Of Post-modernism

Historians should stop behaving as if they are researching into things that actually happened. They should just tell stories without bothering whether or not they are true. As we can never know anything at all about the past, we might as well confine ourselves to studying rival historians. Alternatively, we may dismiss all history as just naked ideology designed to provide historians power and money in big university institutions run by the bourgeoisie. In any case all the world is a text and time is a fictional construct.

Is it really worth to refuting such views from the more extreme of the historians who call themselves post-modernists or occasionally deconstructionists? The professor of modern history at Cambridge, Richard Evans, evidently believes the effort necessary, so entrenched have such people become in universities.

Those of us fortunate enough to be distant from the scene of battle must respect his verdict. Evans certainly hammers the post-modernists into the ground by detailed consideration of their specific arguments and demolition of their logic. He is however willing to give them some due, saying that they have emphasised the importance of looking critically at texts for hidden or unintended meanings. Maybe he is even too generous. For some of the best historians have always employed such scepticism and been self conscious about their own interests and political bias.

Most of the post modernists regard themselves as being on the left. So too does Evans, who castigates them for being so concerned with the deconstruction of texts that they ignore the reality of much suffering and oppression. He also points out how extreme deconstruction can provide comfort for the racialist right, as in various attempts to deny the reality of the Nazi holocaust. I doubt however whether he will convince confirmed practitioners of the new ways. For the rest of us his destruction of postmodernism may be a little wearying, with chapter after chapter and example after example. Indeed the author can do the job in a few lines. For, as he points out, if there is no such thing as truth and we are free to tell what stories we like then there is no particular reason to believe the deconstructionists, who are thus contradicted by their own doctrines.

Perhaps Evans is too much of a historian and not enough of a speculative thinker to ask about the basis of the absurdities which he condemns. They have

* Reprinted from *The Spectator*, 27 September 1997.

at least three separate roots. The first is philosophical scepticism which reflects itself in traditional concerns about our knowledge of other minds, doubts about whether the world exists outside our sensations, and so on. Such scepticism is not as easily debunked as the postwar Oxford linguistic analysts supposed. But it exists on a different plane of discourse from history or the social sciences. To talk about the Napoleonic Wars or the Great Depression or the career of Frederick the Great assumes that there were such things. To investigate history, we have to suspend metaphysical doubt, just as we do in daily life. Nobody recognised this more clearly than that great sceptic, the eighteenth-century Scottish philosopher David Hume, But he set aside his doubts not merely when he wandered into society but when he went on to write a classic history of England which he believed to be something other than a work of his imagination.

A second root of postmodernism is the desire to continue the Marxist critique of western society by other means. Most of the empirical claims of Marxism had been falsified well before the Berlin Wall fell in 1989. Intellectuals who half realised this had to find fresh structures of oppression, whether of race or gender, to replace the old typologies. (Hence pejorative expressions such as "dead white males".) But they also needed to immunise themselves against empirical criticism. Whereas the most endearing feature of old fashioned Marxism was its belief in a happy ending, many postmodernists are mired in a permanent pessimism which will always give them something to deconstruct and undermine.

A third element is the retreat from reason, discernible also in New Age fashions, the indulgence given to medical quacks and the contemporary kind of religiosity stretching from revived fundamentalism to the more fantastic California cults. Alas, we do not have any good general theory explaining these periodic revolts against enlightenment and telling us the conditions in which they flourish or wither.

Fortunately Evans does not confine himself to postmodernism. The most interesting part of his book is the first third in which he outlines the history of history as a discipline. The rival historical schools of the last generation were represented by E H Carr and Sir Geoffrey Elton. At this distance they seem beyond caricature. Carr, the historian of the USSR, believed that history must be governed by a vision of the future, which he took to mean that of Soviet-style collectivism. But he also prided himself in his realism and did not consider the activities of ordinary people merited investigation until the last century or two when organised socialist movements appeared. Elton, by contrast, was a refugee from central Europe who admired not so much English democracy as English order and became a great fan of Thomas Cromwell, the ruthless agent of Henry VIII. Elton asserted, however, that the political views of historians were irrelevant and that the study of sources could be as objective as the analysis of chemical elements.

Evans holds the more balanced view that the interests and beliefs of the historian inevitably affect the story he or she tells. Thus many interpretations are possible, but the honest historian cannot say just what he likes and is confined by evidence.

The Cambridge historian touches on, but does not fully explore, the relationship between history and the social sciences. He mentions the early ambitions of the cliometricians, who wanted to make history a science by applying a mixture of economic theory and modern statistical methods. One notable example was *Time on the Cross*, which its authors believed demonstrated that slavery was an economically viable way of life in the American South – although that could not in the least excuse it morally. But other qualified investigators believe that they have torn the whole edifice to pieces. Modern techniques have thus in no way banished old fashioned controversies but reinstated them in more complex form.

The most perplexing problem raised by *In Defence of History* has little to do with postmodernism. Conventional political and diplomatic history is now only a small fraction of the vast amounts being written. History may be breaking up into thousands of different specialities, which no one person can hope to grasp. The most he or she can learn to do is to tap into selected parts on the Internet. A historian of epidemics is likely to have more in common with a medical scientist interested in this subject than with a student of politics at the time of the accession of George III.

We can say that there is a still a common historical core based on political events in one's own country, to which a selection from other specialities can be added. Or we can say that there longer a single subject history, but a historical aspect to many different disciplines. The choice is a semantic one, but will inevitably be influenced by contemporary politics, whether of the academic variety or the hubris of Ministers of Education who purport to lay down common curricula.

Reference

Evans, R. J., (1997). *In Defence of History*. Cambridge: Granta Books.

PART IV

DIRECTIONS OF ADVANCE

Chapter Eleven
Darwinian Psychology, Political
Economy And The Problem Of Groups*

Introduction

There are several reasons for my interest in recent attempts to extend Darwinism into a more comprehensive explanation of human behaviour and psychology. Over the years I have been put off by being told that various disputes depended on one's view of the "Nature of Man". I used to be a very occasional participant at a seminar held in Interlaken, where the Swiss-American Karl Brunner tried to win German social scientists away from what he called a sociological view of human beings towards an economic one. My own reaction was that the nature of Man was a biological question to be investigated empirically and not a matter for profound armchair theorising. The same applies to the different views of our species held by the eighteenth- and nineteenth-century social theorists brought so vividly to life in the works of Isaiah Berlin.

My interest goes back even earlier. I did once contemplate becoming a professional psychologist, no doubt out of a naive desire to better the human condition and a less naive suspicion that this was unlikely to come about through conventional political action. If I had not been dissuaded from this course by my elders (but not necessarily betters), I would have joined a pretty fragmented discipline. Today's new Darwinian psychology, although still controversial, provides a chance for a more unified point of view.

That is not all. As a matter of temperament, I have been attracted both to individualism and to reductionism. In positive terms this means analysing the behaviour of groups as far as possible in terms of their constituent units. Ethically, it means judging the goals of public policy in terms of their effects on individuals rather than collective abstractions such as "England", "national morale", "the army" or the welfare of a corporate body. Although economic reporting is largely in terms of abstract concepts such as gross national product, unemployment rates, price levels, exchange rates and so on, that is an

* Based on my contribution to G Mulgan (ed), *Life After Politics*, London, Fontana, 1997.

unavoidable vulgarisation. The core of neo-classical economic analysis is in terms of individuals and not societies, however embarrassing many British practitioners find this fact. Neo-Darwinism is even more reductive, conducting its analysis at the level of the gene.

The Neo-Classical Economic Model

A thoughtful discussion of neo-classical economic assumptions is that of Gerard Radnitzky, a German philosopher of science. "Human beings," he writes, "are rational maximisers throughout the whole, or at least a very broad range, of their social interactions". He also refers to a whole string of nouns: scarcity, opportunities, preferences, costs, benefits, competition, rationality, optimality and equilibrium. Behind these formal concepts is the behavioural assumption that Man makes efforts to better his condition. Brunner used to speak of Resourceful, Evaluating, Maximising Man – REMM.

The weakness of the economic model is the uncertainty about what is being maximized. To say "material wellbeing" is too narrow and not always true. Radnitzky emphasizes "the great variety of concrete psychological motivations". Yet a fully comprehensive notion of utility makes the whole exercise circular and drives the subject into an empty mathematical formalism. In practice those economists who bother about such matters assume that most human beings are chiefly concerned with the wellbeing of their closest family and associates, with some margin for more generalised benevolence. But other goals, such as hierarchy and power, do not fit in too easily. Neither do moral goals or constraints which both limit and modify the pursuit of self-chosen interests.

It is no accident that Radnitzky's analysis comes at the beginning of a book he edited, *Universal Economics*. This is one in a series of attempts to present economic theory as a general theory of all human behaviour, explaining not only the financial pages of the newspaper, but every other page as well. Less friendly critics have called it "economic imperialism". The movement seems to me well past its zenith. Its most lasting legacy is that the better economists discuss not only what an ideal policy would be, but what might make governments and other agents actually follow such a policy. For instance there has been a switch of emphasis from specific policy advice to institutional structures like independent central banks or supranational currencies and also to constitutional procedures and voting methods, which are no longer left to traditional political analysts alone.

Paradigms Compared

The Darwinian and neo-classical economic models are ranged together against the sociological model which prevailed until recently and which emphasizes groups such as nations, classes, or occupational interests rather than individuals. The sociological view also plays down innate human characteristics in

favour of the assumption that environmental forces – above all human institutions which are open to change – are the dominant force in determining
behaviour.

Links between evolutionary biology and economics were strong in the
mid-nineteenth century. Darwin paid tribute to Malthus's population theory
as an inspiration for his own "Struggle for Existence". It is known that he had
been reading other classical economists, including Adam Smith, when he first
formulated the basic ideas later to appear in *The Origin of Species.* An
interesting similarity between today's Darwinism and neo-classical economics
remains the postulate of a spontaneous order. Market relations allow a highly
complex division of labour without any central planning mind. Similarly, one
of Darwin's great achievements was to show how the animal and plant world
could develop without the deliberate designer which the theologian William
Paley believed to be necessary.

A spontaneous order is not a perfect one. The most that the invisible hand
explanations can suggest is that human arrangements are not just accidents,
but the result of a long process of intricate change in which unsuccessful
adaptations become jettisoned and successful ones reinforced. The reformer
therefore requires understanding and caution if he or she is to make matters
better rather than worse.

A more subtle contribution of evolutionary theory is to show that change is
more likely to be successful through a series of discrete trial-and-error steps
than through an attempt at one great leap forward. This discovery and error
correction is also something on which the "Austrian" school of economists has
insisted upon – although it can be lost to sight in general equilibrium models.

One obvious difference between many neo-Darwinians and neo-classical
economists is that, as already mentioned, the fundamental unit is the gene in
one case and the individual human being in the other. Yet for some purposes
it makes no difference. The sort of person who is shocked by the remark "There
is no such thing as society; there are only individuals and their families" would
be equally shocked if it concluded instead "There are only genes and their
carriers". Those who can see the point of the remark can equally operate at
either level.

A more basic difference is that a gene is not conscious of its activities and
reference to it as "selfish" or talk of its struggle to reproduce is metaphorical.
A human economic agent, on the other hand, has some consciousness of what
he or she is doing. The Chicago school, and especially Milton Friedman, are
adamant that it does not matter whether people consciously follow their
assumptions. They do not worry whether a businessman is consciously maximising his profits or his utility, so long as his behaviour is best predicted on
such assumptions. Indeed Friedman refers to the differential survival of the
businessman who does maximize.

Nevertheless the economic agent is conscious of something. It is silly to
throw away information on why real businessmen think they are saving,
investing or not taking on more workers – even if we afterwards reinterpret
this information in different terms. Not even the most hard boiled of economic
positivists would want to throw away the surveys of business intentions which

contribute so much to macroeconomic investigation. Another difference is that neo-classical economists theorise about optimality conditions. A lot of high-grade mathematical effort has gone into defining the conditions in which a competitive market equilibrium would yield a social optimum. Evolutionary biologists talk in non-evaluative terms about survival and reproduction. The nearest they approach to the economists' optimality is the notion of an evolutionary stable strategy.

In their full rigour, the economic conditions for optimality are extremely unlikely to occur; and this fact has been used by a subset of general equilibrium theorists to discredit efforts to liberalise markets. But such general equilibrium theorists do not suggest any alternative direction for policy and are in my view near a dead-end. The "Austrian" economists, who see markets as a discovery technique in a world where tastes and techniques are changing and information is scarce and expensive, are much nearer to the evolutionary paradigm.

There is some reason to regard this last paradigm as the primary one. The neo-classical economist thinks of human motivation in terms of material gain or at least the maximisation of choice or utility. The political theorist thinks of power over others. But both power and money may be further analysed as means towards reproductive success. Indeed wealth and power have often been judged by the number of wives, concubines and children a man could have – said to run into many thousands in the case of some east African sultans. Thus the things that the economic agent is said to maximise – whether wealth or utility – may be a side effect of pursuing fundamental biological goals.

It has to be said, however, that the resemblances between neo-classical economics and evolutionary theory are fairly general ones of form. Economists and evolutionary biologists do not cooperate very much and are usually even physically far apart on university campuses. The most successful economic applications of evolutionary ideas have been in areas such as the rise and fall of business firms. There is obvious scope here for metaphors of adaptation, natural selection and the extinction of maladapted species. Even here, however, there is nothing corresponding to the genetic analysis of modern biology. In areas of economics with which I have been most concerned, such as macroeconomics or the comparison of economic systems, there has been little cross-fertilisation. Applications of evolutionary theory to the question of central bank independence or the choice between monetary and exchange rate targets are likely to be highly indirect for the foreseeable future.

There is much argument about whether either or both the economic and the Darwinian models are tautologies. At most, they are weakly falsifiable. Both are open to the charge that almost anything that happens can be interpreted in their terms and that it is difficult to think of any plausible phenomena that they rule out. But the absence of strong falsifiability does not make either model useless. Popper described evolutionary theory as a metaphysical research programme. This was not meant to be a stricture. On the contrary, he regarded such programmes as a source for a great many more specific lower level theories which were indeed falsifiable.

Not all the similarities between economics and Darwinian biology are reassuring. The obsession with the personality of Darwin and what he really thought and meant will be familiar to the political economist accustomed to such discussions about Keynes and others. This is in contrast to physics, where arguments about what Einstein really meant and how he differed from Newton are mainly the province of historians of science.

Evolutionary theory has also brought back Aristotle's teleology – that is, it looks for the purpose and function of objects and processes – which physical science had previously banished. One aspect of it is known as adaptationism. This involves treating any feature, such as a giraffe's neck or the peacock's tail, as an adjustment to some feature of the environment. The method is reminiscent of how Chicago economists treat many phenomena, ranging from the common law to the conventions of family life, as optimal adaptations to the pursuit by human beings of maximum utility. Darwinians accept that some phenomena are just there by an accident of history (genetic drift), but argue that we should always begin by looking for an adaptationist explanation. This is all very well, so long as we realise that adaptation is rarely perfect. As well as the woodpecker's beak, there are residual features such as the vestigial human tail.

One historical accident affected the development of evolutionary theory: the genetic basis of heredity did not become widely known until well after Darwin's death. Darwin himself did not know about chromosomes and genes, let alone the mechanisms by which spontaneous mutations occur, the most successful of which perpetuate themselves in their species. One wonders how the subject would have developed if the historical accident had been the other way round – if the work of Gregor Mendel, who lived in monastic obscurity, had been more widely disseminated in his own lifetime, or if Darwin had written a little later. I sometimes ask how much could be said about human development and characteristics on the basis of genetics and biochemistry without throwing in the notion of purpose or natural selection.

The Neo-Darwinian Approach

A good introduction to Darwinian thinking comes in a quotation from Professor Steve Jones, who is a mainline geneticist:

> Natural selection takes advantage of the fact that in each generation, inheritance makes mistakes. Because some are better at coping with what life throws at them, they copy themselves more successfully. Darwin's mechanism sorts out the best from what mutation supplies. It gives a direction to evolution and allows a living system to escape from the inevitability of extinction. This is as true for humans as for any other creature.

Or as an economist might put it: agents maximise their chances of reproductive success.

"Survival of the fittest" is misleading. Natural selection is concerned with differential reproductive success. Furthermore, selection acts not on an organism but on genes. As Samuel Butler once put it: "A hen is only an egg's way of making another egg". Modern Darwinism rejects group selection. Maxims such as "Nature cares for the species but not for the individual" are now known to be wrong. The species is of interest only to the extent that providing for its welfare helps the gene to reproduce. This leaves room for at least two kinds of altruism: kinship altruism and reciprocal altruism. The first occurs when an organism reduces or sacrifices its own chances of reproduction for the sake of other organisms with which it has some relevant genes in common. J B S Haldane is supposed to have said that he would be prepared to give his life to save two brothers or sisters or eight cousins (although actually he should have been indifferent). Reciprocal altruism is more complicated. The point is that some degree of self sacrifice for the sake of reciprocal advantage is programmed into the behaviour of many organisms on the basis that, if others do the same, their own reproductive chances are maximised.

Reciprocal altruism is usually illustrated by means of the theory of games. Some degree of self sacrifice for the sake of another's benefit may actually pay an organism, provided that others do the same. Then the benefit to a representative member of the whole group is increased. In the case of a herd of antelopes, some form of unconscious programming may lead one antelope to act as a sentinel to warn of the coming of predators. Another notable conclusion is that racial differences are trivial, because the races have separated from each other too recently on the evolutionary timescale. On the other hand, sex differences are fundamental because of the different role of the two sexes in the reproductive process. Because of the length of pregnancy and later care of offspring, a female human has far fewer possibilities of producing offspring than the male – as demonstrated by the prevalence of polygamy in tribal societies. The desire to produce as many offspring as possible accounts for phenomena as diverse as the development of peacock's tails to attract the maximum number of peahens and the aggressive behaviour of young human males which stems from the battle to possess desirable females.[1]

The struggle to exist seems to leave many options open. An equilibrium might be anything from a stable community of a few dozen individuals – such as certain giant lizards – to billions of fellow creatures covering the surface of the earth. Where in between is the definition of success? Perhaps we should follow Matt Ridley (1994) in regarding evolution as a zero sum game. Creatures do not progress. They have to change if they are to keep up, not merely with competition from other creatures, but from competition with their fellows of the same species.

Earlier evolutionary biologists concentrated on physical features and on behaviour. Some modern writers also discuss the accompanying thoughts and feelings, which harks back to some interests of Darwin himself. The idea of human nature has been revived, especially by Matt Ridley and Robert Wright.

Let me mention two striking applications. First, the vast majority of murders are committed by young men – not women – an instance of the struggle to fertilise as many ova as possible. Secondly, instances of child abuse and neglect are far more common among step-parents than natural ones, illustrating the effects of the absence of any genetic relationship. This example confirms the wicked stepmother syndrome, which some may have regarded as a feature of fairy tales or unconscious infantile fears. One implication is that the presumption in favour of the mother having custody of children in divorce cases might be re-examined if the father is prepared to bring up the children himself and if the mother has acquired a new partner. (In Joanna Trollope's *The Choir*, the son of the runaway mother hit on the solution of staying with his maternal grandfather.)

After Eugenics

There are already many practical applications of the new biology to disciplines such as plant and animal breeding and medical science. But what application is there in broader questions about the management of human affairs? It is not surprising that early attempts to improve the human race should have given the whole idea a bad name. Jones, a geneticist who is highly critical of the eugenics movement, has given numerous unfortunate examples. Francis Galton started the eugenics drive in part to "check the birth rate of the unfit and improve the race by furthering the activity of the fit by early marriage of the best stock". Winston Churchill expressed similar sentiments when he was Home Secretary in 1910, but they were not made public until 1992. It is notorious that Hitler carried such thinking to the extent of concentration camps and to experiments on living people. Elisabeth Nietzsche, the sister of the philosopher, chose what she regarded as especially splendid German volunteers to start a community in Paraguay in 1886 that would be the beginning of a new race of supermen and women. In the late twentieth century, the remaining survivors of Nueva Germania have been found to be poor, inbred and diseased.

Such enthusiasms were by no means confined to the political right. The central theme of Bernard Shaw's *Man and Superman* was the admission that contemporary men and women were not equipped to make a go of socialism, but to conclude that the species must be improved until they could. This becomes very clear in the appendix entitled *The Revolutionist's Handbook?*. He writes:

> The only fundamental and possible socialism is the socialistion of the selective breeding of Man; in other terms of human evolution. We must eliminate the Yahoo or his vote will wreck the Commonwealth . . . that may mean that we must establish a State Department of Evolution, with a seat in the Cabinet for its chief, and a revenue to defray the cost of direct state experiments and provide inducements to private persons to achieve successful results.

These examples show not only that schemes for genetic improvement are peculiarly liable to manipulation by evil people. They also show the danger of jumping the gun, that is, of acting before knowledge in this highly emotive area is really secure. We must therefore be grateful that Shaw and Galton – who were far from evil men – were not able to give full rein to their fancies.

We cannot retreat forever from ideas because they have been misunderstood and interpreted in absurd ways. The fact that a certain form of behaviour has genetic roots does not mean that it has to be modified genetically. Different results will be produced by the same genetic material under different environmental conditions. Caution suggests that the overwhelming emphasis of any attempts at improvement deriving from Darwinian psychology should be directed at the institutional environment which interacts with innate tendencies.

But can we be sure that this will always be enough? Can we honestly and for ever rule out a more directly genetic approach? This is already a central feature of discussions about preventing the most dreadful inborn diseases. But would it not be a gain to have human beings whose innate programming made them less likely to indulge in actions like ethnic cleansing?

It should not be controversial to say that there are many profoundly distasteful aspects of the behaviour of the human species. One need only to point to events in central Africa, the Caucasus, former Yugoslavia or the numerous horrifying examples of child cruelty and child neglect nearer home. Such events crop up in so many forms throughout human history and so far seem impervious to modification by the various forms of political organisation under which people have lived. Their roots must run pretty deep in the nature of the species; and any attempts at improvement would have to be carried out by members of the same species.

Most recent attempts to apply neo-Darwinism to current problems have been in areas like human mating. Characteristic titles of recent papers have been on the evolution of desire and monogamy, polygamy and serial divorce. The avoidance of headline prescriptions for national and international policy reflects a healthy caution after the experiences of the eugenics movement and after the fierce hostility (whether merited or not) which greeted E O Wilson's attempt to launch "sociobiology" in the mid-1970s.

Philosophical critics object to the use of words like hypocrisy in some popular Darwinian books to describe apparently noble attitudes which can be traced to basic survival strategies, like kin altruism and reciprocal altruism. As a matter of logic the critics are right: a man who jumps into a raging torrent to save a child is not a hypocrite, whether his actions spring from genetic programming, the effects of events in his early infancy or anything else. Yet if we are interested in promoting such acts or minimising other anti-social ones, the more we can learn about their origins the better.

Groups

Finally let me note, without trying to solve, what has struck me again and again as the most difficult problem posed by human evolution. During 98 per cent of its past existence the human species is said to have lived in small bands of around 100 to 150 hunter gatherers, usually closely related to each other. The nature of such groups is illuminated by the colourful idea of a tribal chief who would periodically be killed by a younger male who would then take on the role of leadership himself, a primordial Oedipal event of which there are, according to some, still traces in the modern adult human mind. The impact of these early groups has been pondered over by thinkers as different as Sigmund Freud and Friedrich Hayek.

Romantic beliefs about the superior behaviour of primitive groups uncorrupted by civilisation are neatly punctured by a modern anecdote. Vice President Albert Gore of the US likes to quote from a moving speech supposedly uttered by Chief Seattle in 1854 when the US government offered to buy his land.

> The earth is our mother. What befalls the earth befalls all parts of the earth. The earth does not belong to man, man belongs to the earth.

It later transpired that the entire speech was written for an ABC television drama by screenwriter Ted Perry in 1971. The real Chief Seattle was a slave owner who had killed most of his enemies.(Details are to be found in Ridley, 1997).

It is extremely unlikely that the behaviour that emerged through natural selection in the population of hunter gatherers would in all respects be suitable for today's Great Society. The good side of group solidarity is obvious enough: family affection, patriotism, mutual help, doing one's duty and all the communitarian virtues. So, alas, is the bad side: intolerance of the outsider, willingness to go to war for trivial reasons, ethnic cleansing, football hooliganism and much else.

The syndrome is often much discussed under the heading of nationalism or xenophobia. But that is to understate it. People of the most diverse nationalities sacrificed their lives for the British Empire, the Hapsburg Empire and many others. When there are no genuine national differences or rival crowns, religious differences will do instead. Indeed the most trivial distinction will divide people into ferociously hostile factions. In Imperial Constantinople a completely artificial distinction between blues and greens, factions at the circus, divided the population into groups whose hostility could lead to murder and worse.

There is another aspect to in-group feelings of which honesty compels a mention. That is the hostility to any reward system depending on the luck of the market rather than face-to-face evaluation. This can do untold damage to the reward and incentive structure on which the market depends. To protect my flank, I must point out there it may be possible to redistribute income via the tax and transfer system to those ill-favoured by the market. The harm that is done is in the resistance to equilibrium rates of pay, so that some people are priced out of work while other types of worker are in short supply.

Market-inclined economists often say their opponents want to pay according to supposed "merit" or are over-influenced by egalitarianism. But this may not be quite right. People in face-to-face groups do not look for either equality or moral merit in scales of pay. They look for a known and agreed hierarchy which does not change too quickly. Is it possible that these responses reflect the hunter-gatherer group, which had agreed rules for the sharing of prey? What is more difficult to explain is why very large prizes which depend completely on luck – such as those distributed in the National Lottery – or mostly on luck – as in the case of popular entertainers and sportsmen – are nevertheless acceptable.

One recent attempt at explaining group hostilities is related by Steven Pinker (1997). In foraging societies men go to war to get or keep women. Put in a sentence, this sounds like a sick joke. But the mechanism has been described in some detail with some explanation, for instance, of how and when the warlike spirit is most likely to be inflamed, when war weariness is likely to develop and why most people are reluctant to send women into combat.

Conclusion

The two problems of group mentality – (a) resistance to the market rewards which emerge from the Great Society and (b) the enormously powerful drive of such groups to make war on, or otherwise oppress, other groups – have haunted me for a long time. Both kinds of behaviour are examples of people thinking that they are rising above self-interest when they are actually falling below it, and produce results which are worse than the pursuit of genuine self-interest constrained by a framework of rules and customary inhibitions. In the time-honoured tradition of suggesting work for other people to do, I hope that the next crop of Darwinian investigations will go into detail on this tribal legacy and make specific suggestions on how we can either modify it or live with it without blowing ourselves to pieces.

Appendix: The Bogey of Determinism

Any attempt at a scientific or semi-scientific explanation of human behaviour – whether Darwinian, Freudian or anything else – comes up against the charge of determinism. If our actions are determined by some combination of genetic endowment and the environment, does not free will go out of the window; and what becomes of traditional notions of blame and punishment?

The view that behaviour can be entirely accounted for by heredity and environment is part of a metaphysical research programme. But let us suppose that, however far science advances, there will continue to be an element in behaviour not predictable from prior information and that we will have to be content with the "interpretations" explained towards the end of Chapter Nine. Does that reintroduce free will? Surely not. Free will, for those who believe in it, is not randomness but conscious control over one's destiny. The same applies to the indeterminate elements in modern quantum mechanics. If an electron unpredictably jumps from one circuit to another, or if it is impossible to measure precisely the mass of a particle together with its velocity, the particles in question still do not exhibit anything in the least like the power to determine their conduct that God supposedly gave to human beings. Someone who is inclined to doubt whether anyone is ever to "blame" is on equally strong ground whatever the proportions of predictability and randomness in human affairs.

I am reinforced in this conclusion by learning that Hume had already reached it more than two centuries ago. "Hume's Fork" is a name sometimes given to the assertion that "either our actions are determined, in which case we are not responsible for them; or they are the result of random events, in which case we are also not responsible for them" (*Oxford Dictionary of Philosophy*). As this is something I have believed all my life, it only serves to confirm my admiration for Hume. In more recent years, A J Ayer remarked that this intelligence has profound implications for our attitude to blame and crime.

Many people feel that without free will there would be no case for personal or political freedom. Wrong. My freedom to travel to Iceland means that no one will stop me. It is not affected by whether some scientist with enough data about my genetic constitution and all past events in my life could predict whether I would choose to make the journey. The opposite of freedom is coercion, not determinism.

Determinism, properly understood, is a humane doctrine which substitutes understanding for judgement and limits punishment to where it is unavoidable as a deterrent. It is those who go on about free will and responsibility who are most inclined to clamour for retributive justice. Indeed as Wright suggests, the illusion about free will could be an adaptation. In practice a person is said to have free will if anticipations of punishment can influence him – or, an economist might say, if he responds to incentives. If no praise or blame or sanctions have the slightest chance of affecting a person's actions, courts are likely to accept that his crime was committed as a result of some psychotic disorder. The court decision does not imply an absence of genetic and environmental causality, but merely that the accused is not affected by normal human incentives. Free will and its absence are convenient fictions, as is the doctrine that anyone ever deserves anything. In Wright's words, we have to live with the intellectual groundlessness of blame and the practical use for it.

References

Ayer, A. J., (1982). *Philosophy in the 20th Century*: pp 16–17. London: Unwin Paperback

Badcock, C., (1994). *PsychoDarwinism*. London: HarperCollins.

Blackburn, S., (1996). *Oxford Dictionary of Philosophy*. Oxford: University Press.

Cronin, H., (1991). *The Ant and the Peacock*. Cambridge: Publisher?

Dawkins, R., (1989). *The Selfish Gene*. Revised edn. Oxford: Oxford University Press.

Jones, S., (1994). *The Language of the Genes*. London: HarperCollins.

Pinker, S., (1994). *The Language Instinct*. London: Penguin.

Pinker, S., (1998). *How The Mind Works*. London: Allen Lane.

Popper, K. R., (1976). *Unended Quest*. London: Fontana.

Ridley, M., (1994). *The Red Queen*. London: Penguin.

Ridley, M., (1997). *The Origins of Virtue*. London: Viking.

Radnitzky, G., (ed.) (1992), *Universal Economics*. New York: Pergamon House.

Wright, R., (1995). *The Moral Animal*. London: Little Brown.

Notes

Chapter 5
1. *Freedom in the Modern World*, pp 194–197.

Chapter 7
1. I owe this formulation to Peter Jay.
2. *Pop Internationalism*, cited in previous chapter.

Chapter 8
1. This refers to his academic writings. He was not successful as Austrian Finance Minister after World War One.
2. Based on personal conversation with Friedman.

Chapter 9
1. Treatise Part I, Chapter XIV, p.162.
2. A J Ayer, (1980).
3. Explained in Peter Kennedy (1992).
4. The clearest and most up to date account of Friedman's teachings on the relation of money to inflation and economic fluctuation is to be found in chapter 2 of *Monetary Mischief* (1992). The book has not had the attention it deserves, perhaps because it is neither polemic nor technical tract.
5. Named after some obiter dicta by Professor Charles Goodhart, a former Bank of England economist, and subsequently a founder member of its Monetary Policy Committee.
6. This section is indebted to Basu (1981).

Chapter 11
1. I have no intention of getting diverted into feminist issues. But as a matter of logic, one must emphasise that different does not mean inferior. Socialists of an earlier era, such as Douglas Jay, used to stress that they thought that human beings were worthy of equal respect – which did not mean that they had equal abilities. It was only with the later degeneration

of these ideas that egalitarianism was taken to require the denial of human differences of which every mother is aware. Similarly, emphasis on male and female differences does not mean that one sex is superior to the other. Nor does it mean that every male or female will exhibit characteristics typical of the sex. It is more that the frequency distribution of characteristics will be around different means. If I dare invoke what was once a neutral technical term: the bell curves will be in different places.